Meyrick's Medieval Knights and Armour

Samuel Rush Meyrick

Dover Publications, Inc., Mineola, New York

Bibliographical Note

This Dover edition, first published in 2007, contains the Introduction and all full-page plates from the second edition of *A Critical Inquiry into Antient Armour, as It Existed in Europe, Particularly in Great Britain, from the Norman Conquest, to the Reign of King Charles II,* published in three volumes by Henry G. Bohn, London, 1842. The "Comparative Table" of geographical names originally presented at the end of the Introduction has been omitted from this edition. In addition, the color plates have been renumbered, from 1 to 71.

International Standard Book Number:

ISBN-13: 978-0-486-45751-2
ISBN-10: 0-486-45751-6

Manufactured in the United States of America
Dover Publications, Inc., 31 East 2nd Street, Mineola, N.Y. 11501

INTRODUCTION.

Armour had its origin in Asia, the warlike tribes of Europe at first contemned all protection but their innate courage, and considered any defence except the shield as a mark of effeminacy. The warm climate of Asia, however, together with its temptations to luxury, had too great a tendency to enervate its inhabitants, so that, to be on an equality with their neighbours, they were obliged to have recourse to artificial protection. As all the European armour, except the plate, which was introduced at the close of the fourteenth century, was borrowed from the Asiatics, it becomes necessary, towards its thorough elucidation, to give some introductory account of their antient armour.

ASIATIC ARMOUR.

In considering the subject, I must be allowed to bring under this head the armour of the Egyptians, for though their country is not precisely in Asia, yet their habits were Asiatic, and different from those of the Africans, and their intercourse with Asia was so frequent and early, that I should think it a useless distinction to separate them.

EGYPTIAN ARMOUR.

Notwithstanding the effeminate character given to the Egyptians by Herodotus, we have reason to conclude, that in the earliest periods of their history, they had obtained some renown for their martial achievements. The battles of Sesostris, Asymanduas, and Xamolxis, though merely mythological, and referring to the propagation of particular religious tenets, would not have been represented under a military character, had it not at the time most suited the genius of the people. Herodotus tells us what were the arms and armour of the Egyptians, the helmet of Psammeticus was of brass, but metal was confined to kings and nobles, for the soldiery wore them of linen, strongly quilted, a fashion continued by the sailors so late as the time of Xerxes, who employed them in his expedition into Greece. The only body armour was the pectoral, which hung over the breast and shoulders like a tippet, this was made of linen several times folded, and quilted in such a manner as to resist the point of a weapon, it was of various colours, and one presented by Amasis, the king of Egypt, to the Lacedemonians, is said to have been adorned with many figures of animals, and enriched with gold. The chain was of admirable structure, fine and slender, although consisting of 363 distinct threads, that being a mystical number, viz., the number of days in the antient year, and, consequently, supposed to contain a charm. Such another, presented by the same king, was to be seen at Lindus, dedicated to Minerva. The warriors had likewise shields, which, in the time of Xerxes, were convex and, as weapons, a short sword and a javelin. The troops who fought in the ships had merely large daggers, while their commanders had javelins and immense double-axes. The ornaments of the warriors were torques and bracelets. From the Old Testament, we further learn, that war-chariots were used in great numbers by the kings of Egypt.

On the walls of the temple of Carnac are several representations of conquests, in which we have the armour, weapons, standards, and chariots of the Egyptians, but these bear so very strong a resemblance to Grecian workmanship, that there is no doubt of their having been painted during the Ptolomean dynasty.[1] They are engraved in Plate LXXIII of Denon's Egypt. There is, too, a military triumph at a temple near Medinet-Abou, represented in Plate LXXIV of Denon, and several paintings of arms and armour, on the walls of a chamber in the tombs of the kings at Thebes. The Greek helmet, the shield, which, from its resemblance to a gate, being oblong and curved at top, they called *Θυρέος*, and the Grecian chariot, strike us at once, but the only body armour is the Egyptian pectoral. The colours of this last we learn from a painting discovered at Herculaneum, and published in the Antichite d'Ercolano, as we do those of the helmet, which appears to have had a kind of tiara or ornamented frontlet. We learn moreover, from Denon's engraving, that this thureos was carried by putting the spear through the aperture made for looking at their enemies; and also, that the quiver for lances, and the quiver for arrows, were put on each side the car, or across each other on one side, the warrior not only using his bow, but driving the horses, the reins being fastened round his waist. But the most curious painting on these walls, if correctly delineated, is a tunic of rings, set edgewise, or single mail, as it was afterwards called in Europe, as this is the earliest specimen of that species of hauberk.[2] Mr. Hope also, from Denon, has given the figure as he supposes of a priest, habited in a cuirass of scales, which comes up to the armpits, and is there held by shoulder-straps.

Plate I. contains specimens of these Græco-Egyptian arms and armour. Fig. 1. A cutting sword, with cord and tassel at the hilt, a practice still in fashion among the Persians. Fig. 2. A scymitar, with double cord to the hilt. Fig. 3. A long dagger in its sheath, with double cord, its general resemblance, particularly in the hilt, to the Moorish and Turkish daggers of the present day is strikingly curious. Fig. 4. A mace, with a guard for the hand. Fig. 5. The shield called Thureos. Fig. 6. A military pectoral. Fig. 7. and 8. Helmets. Fig. 9. The padded linen cap worn by the soldiery. Fig. 10. and 11. Helmets. Fig. 12. Military cap of a charioteer. Fig. 13. A quiver containing javelins, with a throwing stick. Fig. 14. The throwing stick taken out of the quiver. Fig. 15. A quiver for arrows, with its covering. Fig. 16. An arrow. Fig. 17. A spear. Fig. 18. A battle-axe, rendered heavier by a weight on the back of the blade. Fig. 19. Another battle-axe. Fig. 21. and 22. Standards. Fig. 22. Denon's incorrect representation of the body armour.

Since the first edition of this critical enquiry the systematic work of Sir Gardiner Wilkinson has made its appearance, the result of twelve years residence in Egypt, and a thorough investigation of the Egyptian remains brought to this country. At the hazard therefore of tautology, the following condensed remarks are added.

The strength of the army consisted in archers, they fought either on foot or in chariots, and may therefore be classed under the separate heads of a mounted and unmounted corps, and they probably constituted the chief part of both wings. Several bodies of heavy infantry divided into regiments, each distinguished by its peculiar arms, formed the centre; and the cavalry, which according to the Scriptural accounts was numerous, covered, and supported the foot; and they had also mercenary troops, who were enrolled either from the nations in alliance with the Egyptians, or from those who

[1] It was, however, suggested to me, by my learned friend, Mr. Douce, that this may merely indicate that which the Greeks borrowed, for both they and the Romans left the Egyptians so much to themselves, as never to have erected a temple for their own forms of worship.

[2] I find this doubt fully confirmed by the very valuable publication of Sir Gardiner Wilkinson, for in the 1st Vol. of his "Manners and Customs of the Egyptians," Pl. III, we have it correctly represented, and consisting of about eleven horizontal rows of metal plates well secured by bronze pins.

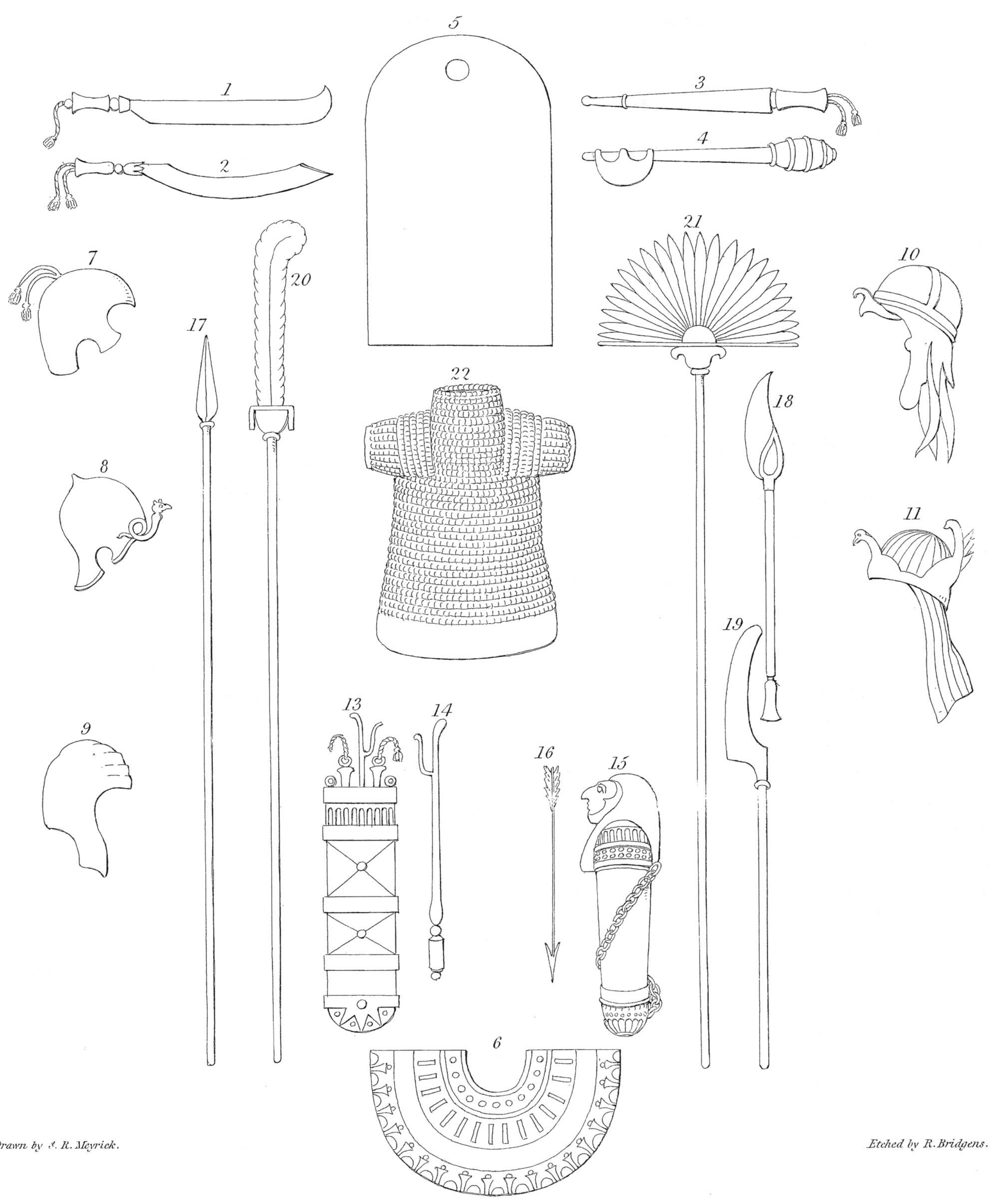

Drawn by S. R. Meyrick. Etched by R. Bridgens.

GRÆCO EGYPTIAN ARMS AND ARMOUR.

had been conquered by them. Masses of heavy infantry armed with spears and shields, and a falchion or other weapon, moved sometimes in close array in the form of an impregnable phalanx, each company having its particular standard, which represented a holy subject, a king's name, a sacred boat, an animal, or some emblematic device. The troops were summoned by sound of trumpet, and this instrument as well as the long drum was used by the Egyptians at the earliest period into which the sculptures have given us an insight, trumpeters being frequently represented in the battle scenes of Thebes, sometimes standing still and summoning the troops to form, and at others in the act of leading them to a rapid charge.

The offensive weapons were the bow, spear, two species of javelin, a sling, a short and straight sword, dagger, knife, falchion, axe or hatchet, battle-axe, pole-axe, mace or club, and the lissan which is a curved stick similar to that still in use among the Ababdeh and modern Ethiopians. Their defensive arms consisted of a helmet of metal, or quilted headpiece, a cuirass or coat of armour, made of metal plates, or quilted with metal bands, and an ample shield. But they had no greaves, and the only coverings to the arms were a part of the cuirass, forming a short sleeve, and extending about half way to the elbow.

The shield was in length equal to half the height of the soldier, and generally double its own breadth. It was most commonly covered with bull's hide, having the hair outwards like the λαισηιον of the Greeks, sometimes strengthened by one or more rims of metal, and studded with nails or metal pins, the inner part being probably wicker work, or a wooden frame. To the inside was attached a thong, by which it was suspended on a man's shoulder. The handle is placed sometimes perpendicularly, sometimes horizontally, and at others so situated that a man might pass his arm through and grasp a spear. The object of a circular cavity in the upper part of the shield, is by no means clear. There are some few instances of a pavoise, or large shield reaching from the shoulder to the ground, and which instead of being semicircular at top, more nearly resembled a Gothic arch.

The Egyptian bow was from five feet to five and a half in length, and was strung by fixing the lower point in the ground, and standing or seated, the knee pressed against the inner side, while it was bent with one hand inwards, the string being passed by the other into the notch at the upper extremity. The archer wore a brace, which was not only fastened round the wrist, but secured by a thong tied above the elbow. The mode of drawing was either with the forefinger and thumb, or two forefingers, and though in the chase they sometimes brought the arrow merely to the chest, their custom in war was to draw it to the ear. The bow-string, was of hide, catgut, or string, and so great was their confidence in the strength of it, and of the bow, that an archer from his car sometimes used them to entangle his opponent, whilst he smote him with a sword. Their arrows were of wood, or reed, tipped with metal heads, one of which is in the Doucean Museum at Goodrich Court, and they were winged with feathers. They varied in length from 22 to 34 inches. The spear or pike was between five and six feet in length, of wood with a blade of metal into which it was inserted and fixed with nails, as appears in the specimen preserved in the Museum at Berlin.

The javelin was also of wood armed with a two-edged metal head of an elongated diamond shape, either flat, or increasing in thickness at the centre, and sometimes tapering to a very long point. The butt end of the shaft was terminated by a bronze knob, surmounted by a ball, to which were attached two thongs. The sling was a thong of leather or plaited string. The sword was short, straight, and apparently with a double edge, tapering the whole way to a point. The dagger was worn in a leathern sheath, one being preserved in the Museum at Berlin. The axes were often highly ornamented, and some were much in the form of the Indian elephant blades.

LYBIAN ARMOUR.

I SHOULD not have noticed these savages of Africa, who merely carried wooden lances, pointed and hardened at the end by fire, and daubed their bodies with vermilion, had not Herodotus told us,[1] that from them the Greeks received the apparel and ægis of Minerva, as represented upon her images: he, however, observes that there was this difference, that instead of a pectoral of scale armour, in Lybia, it was merely a skin, and that the fringe was of leather instead of serpents. In all other respects, he observes, the resemblance is perfect, and that even the name testifies that it came from Lybia, for the women of that country wear a mantle of tanned goat-skin, dyed red, and fringed,[2] over the rest of their garments. On a fictile vase, in Sir Wm. Hamilton's collection,[3] the figure of Minerva has not only this pectoral of scales, but it has flap sleeves of the same; and on another[4] the ægis is similarly formed, but apparently of quilted instead of scaled work.

The Lybians, Numidians, and Getulians, according to Strabo,[5] and the Massylians, according to Lucan[6] rode without saddles.

ETHIOPIAN ARMOUR.

Mr. Hope says, that the antient Egyptians are evidently descended from the Ethiopians, and gives many physiological reasons for this assertion, I ought not, therefore, wholly to pass over this people. Herodotus tells us, that the manners and habits of the Eastern Ethiopians were greatly analogous to those of the Egyptians, but the western parts of Ethiopia were inhabited by a people much less cultivated. Their shields were often made of the raw hides of oxen. Those who inhabited the parts above Egypt were clothed in the skins of lions or leopards, and, previous to their engagement in battle, they daubed one half of their bodies over with a kind of white plaster, λνψῳ, and painted the other half with vermilion, μιλτῳ. They had bows four cubits long, with arrows proportionate, and pointed with sharp stones instead of iron, and the heads of their javelins were made of goat's horns sharpened: they had also maces armed with iron. The women of this country, moreover, bore arms until they arrived at a certain age.

The dress of the Asiatic Ethiopians had some resemblance to that of the Indians, who used a species of armour made of wood:[7] but instead of a helmet they substituted the skin of a horse's head, stripped from the carcase, together with the ears and mane, and so contrived that the mane served for a crest, while the ears appeared erect upon the head of the wearer.[8] Their shields, unlike those in common use, were composed of the skins of cranes. The people who lived west of the Garamantes wore the skins of ostriches instead of armour. Those who inhabited the isles of the Red Sea were armed like the Medes.

JEWISH ARMOUR.

We have little more than mere names to assist our researches respecting the military habits of the Israelites. Their knowledge of tactics was probably derived from the Egyptians, and, it must be confessed, that they do not appear to have been by any means deficient in military skill at the time they resided in the wilderness. In the latter part of their history they probably adopted many customs of the Syrians. The thorax or pectoral, the plaited girdles for the body, the military sagum or cloak, called an habergeon in our translation of the Pentateuch, together with the helmet, and the shields, which are of two kinds, the one larger than the other, formed the chief part, if not the whole, of their defensive armour. Their offensive arms consisted of swords, some of which had two edges; daggers, spears, javelins, bows, arrows, and slings. Axes or maces, as מפצ should perhaps be trans-

1 Polymnia.

2 Ægis signifies goat-skin.

3 Vol. III, Pl. 49, of the Etruscan Antiquities.

4 Vol. IV, Pl. 12, of the Etruscan Antiquities.

5 Lib. XVII.

6 Lib. IV.

7 Armour of this material is still worn by the Tchutski. See a plate, representing one, in Sauer's Account of Billing's Voyage. There is also in the South Sea room at Goodrich Court a very beautiful cuirass made of pieces of wood, which formed the body-armour of one of the people of the Sitia Isles on the N. W. coast of America.

8 This will lead us to the origin of crests and tufts on helmets.

lated, were also used as weapons of war. The Jewish slingers, indeed, are said to have been so expert, that seven hundred of them in one army could sling stones at a hair's breadth, and not miss.[1] Their weapons appear to have been made of brass, and of iron or steel, for the original word admits of both interpretations, נשק בדזל, a weapon of iron or steel,[2] קשת נחושה, a bow of brass.[3] We also read of shields of gold, that is, probably, plated with gold, for we may easily conceive they would have been much too rich for common use if they had been made entirely of that metal. Although the shields and targets which Solomon caused to be made and hung up in his palace, were of massy gold, yet they appear to have been merely ornamental.[4] The Hebrew word for the thorax, or pectoral, is שרין or שריון, from שרה, to be strong; and, probably, the same kind of armour is meant by Jeremiah, who uses the word סריון, or in the plural, סרינות, from the verb סר, to turn aside, as the armour does the point of the weapon.[5] The pectoral is a part of body armour, exceedingly antient, and which probably originated in Egypt, it is not unlikely, therefore, that the Israelites derived its usage from that country. It is usually called, in the English translation of the Old Testament, a coat of mail, and probably, in remote times, it was attached to a short tunic, in the same manner that the sacred breast-plate was fastened upon the ephod, resembling, in Strutt's idea, the *χιτων χαλκεος*, or brazen vest, mentioned by Homer.[6] Beneath the pectorals were belts plated with brass or other metal, and the uppermost of them was bound upon the bottom of the tunic, which connected the pectoral with the belts, and all of them together formed a tolerably perfect armour for the front of the whole body. These belts, in the Hebrew, are called והנו, and were generally two, one above the other, and appear similar to what are represented in antient Greek sculpture, though in some degree higher upon the breast. This mode of arming perfectly explains the passage in Scripture, where Ahab is said to have been smitten with an arrow בין הדבקים between the openings, or joints, that is, of the belts, ובין השרין and between the thorax or pectoral.[7] The pectorals of the Egyptians were made of linen, and perhaps, antiently, those of the Jews were the same. In after times they seem to have been covered with plates of metal; and, in the New Testament, we meet with the words *θωρακας σιδηρυς*, or pectorals of iron.[8]

The military sagum, or cloak, is called, in our translation, an habergeon, but the original word תחרא is of doubtful signification, and occurs only twice, "And there shall be a hole in the top in the midst thereof;" that is, the robe of the ephod: "it shall have a binding of woven work round about the hole of it, as it were the hole of an *habergeon*, that it be not rent."[9] But of whatever kind the garment may have been, it appears that it had an aperture at the upper part of it, through which the head was passed when it was put upon the body. Mr. Strutt conjectures that it was the tunic upon which the thorax was fastened, and bore the same relation to the thorax that the ephod did to the sacred pectoral.

There were two sorts of helmets in use among the Jewish warriors, at least the helmets are distinguished by two different names, כובע and קובע. They are both said to have been made of brass,[10] but their form is totally unknown: the helmet belonging to the Israelitish monarch was distinguished from those of his subjects by the crown which was placed upon it.[11]

There are four kinds of shields specified in holy writ, their form is no where described, but it is certain that they differed in their size. "King Solomon made two hundred צנה targets of beaten gold, six hundred shekels of gold went to one target: and three hundred מגנים shields of beaten gold, three pounds of gold went to one shield," &c.[12] Hence it is evident, that the צנה was larger than the מגן, the שלטים in one passage seems to have been the same as the מגנים, "there hang a thousand

[1] Judges, ch. xx, v. 16.
[2] Job, ch. xx, v. 24.
[3] Ibid., and Psalm xviii, v. 34.
[4] 1 Kings, ch. x, v. 16, 17.
[5] Jeremiah, ch. xlvi, v. 4 : and ch. xl, v. 3.
[6] Iliad, l. xiii, line 439.
[7] 1 Kings, ch. xxii, v. 34 ; 2 Chron. ch. xviii, v. 33.
[8] Revelations, ch. ix, v. 9.
[9] Exod. ch. xxviii, v. 32 ; and ch. xxxix, v. 23.
[10] 1 Sam. ch vii, v. 5, 38, &c
[11] 2 Sam. ch. i, v. 10.
[12] 1 Kings, ch, x, v. 16 and 17.

המגן bucklers, all שלטי shields of mighty men."[1] The סחרה is a small shield or buckler, "His truth shall be thy צנה shield and סחרה buckler."[2] From the expression of Isaiah, "Arise ye princes, and *anoint* the shields,"[3] some have thought that the Israelites possessed the art of making their shields with leather, or raw hides, but the use of oil would be equally proper if they were covered with brass, to keep them from rusting, and to make them bright.

The offensive weapons, which are only mentioned by name in the sacred writings, did not probably differ from those in use among other Asiatic nations. The sword was usually girded upon the thigh, as we learn from the expression frequently used in Scripture, "Gird every man his sword upon his thigh," whence, it appears, that they did not wear the sword continually, but only when the exigency of the times required the use of such weapons, and that they were suspended in front in the Asiatic style.

ARMOUR OF THE PHILISTINES.

From the description of the arms belonging to Goliath, the giant of Gath, we learn what were those of the Philistines; they consisted of a helmet, a coat of mail, greaves, a small and large shield, a spear, and a sword. The helmet was made of brass כובע נחשת,[4] and is not otherwise particularized; but the cuirass consisted of plates of brass, laid over each other in the form of scales, which is expressed by a word in the original Hebrew, that is totally omitted in our translation, this is קשקשים, scales, which, with the word שריון, is properly rendered by Espenius, Lorica Squamarum. In the Vulgate, this is called Lorica hamata, a cuirass of rings hooked into each other: but the former interpretation agrees best with the original word. The weight of this coat of armour was 5,000 shekels of brass, or about 189 lbs. troy weight. Shining plates of brass מצחת נחשת[5] are expressly said to have been upon his feet על רגלין,[6] but whether these extended over any part of the leg does not appear. He was provided with two shields, the smaller of which he bore between his shoulders, that is, slung probably at his back by a strap, whence he could easily take it, if required, in time of action: the larger one was carried before him by his armour-bearer. His spear was headed with iron, and seems to have been remarkable only for its size, the head weighing 600 shekels, or about 22 lbs. troy weight. The materials from which his sword, and the sheath belonging to it, were fabricated, are not specified, the sword, indeed appears to have been of excellent workmanship, for, it is said, there was none like it, but its size was hardly in proportion to the rest of his arms, for David, at a future period, made use of it instead of his own.

In the time of the Emperor Aurelianus, several of the inhabitants of Palestine served as horse soldiers in the pay of the Romans; and Zosimus tells us, that the cavalry of Palestine, besides other arms, wielded clubs and maces, which they used so effectually on the brass and iron armour of the Palmyrenes, that they broke it in pieces.

PHŒNICIAN ARMOUR.

Such of this nation as accompanied Xerxes, we learn from Herodotus, had helmets upon their heads nearly resembling those worn by the Greeks, and pectorals of quilted linen upon their breasts,[7] which they probably derived from the Egyptians, and if so, this people may be considered as the connecting link, in point of military costume, between those nations. Their roving habits, which made them the best sailors of their time, was doubtless the occasion of this, and as they peopled Carthage and some

1 Canticles, c. IV, v. 4.
2 Psalm XCI, v. 4.
3 Ch. XXI, v. 5.
4 1 Sam. ch. XVII, v. 5.
5 Ibid. v. 6.
6 1 Sam. ch. XVII, v. 6.
7 In Polymnia.

of the ports of Spain, they probably carried thither their antient armour and weapons. Herodotus adds, that they were armed with javelins, and carried round shields without any protuberance at the centre. He does not, however, tell of what metal their arms were fabricated, but from the great trade in tin, which they carried on with Britain, we can have little doubt that they were of a compound metal made from that and copper. This is further confirmed by the Carthaginian swords dug up on the plains of Cannæ, and now in the British Museum, and from the fact, that they introduced this manufacture into Britain, Ireland, and, indeed, wherever they had any dealings.

CARTHAGINIAN ARMOUR.

The Carthaginians, though a warlike nation, raised but few troops from among their own citizens. By means of their riches they drew from various countries soldiers ready disciplined, and of the greatest merit and reputation. From Numidia they derived an active, bold, impetuous, and indefatigable cavalry, which formed the principal strength of their armies; from the Balearian isles the most expert slingers; from Spain a strong and determined infantry; from the coast of Genoa and Gaul troops of known valour; and from Greece itself soldiers fit for all the various operations of war, for the field or garrisons, for besieging or defending cities.

It is difficult, therefore, to assign any armour as peculiar to the Carthaginians, and in no author of antiquity, as far as my researches go, is any such described. In Mr. Bullock's Museum, was a helmet, said to have been found at Carthage, greatly resembling the morians antiently worn in Europe: it was, therefore, much like one in the Hamilton collection of the British Museum, which appears to have been formed by being cast in a mould, and is given Pl. vi, Fig. 4.[1] There are, in the same collection, several brass swords, which General Vallancey says, were found in the plains of Cannæ, and greatly resemble those dug up in Ireland, he, therefore, concludes, they are Carthaginian, and, it is probable, that the helmet may have been found with them. In the Thesaurus Græcorum Antiquitatum of Gronovius, Vol. III, is a silver coin exhibiting a head of Hamilcar Barcas, and another of Hannibal, both of which are quite in the Greek style, but it is now quite clear that there are no genuine coins of Hamilcar or Hannibal.

ARABIAN ARMOUR.

Herodotus observes, that the Arabs carried long bows, made with a handle and two curved horns.

SYRIAN ARMOUR.

The Syrians who inhabited Palestine, at least such of them as went in the expedition of Xerxes, by sea, in order to invade Greece, were, according to Herodotus, armed precisely like the Phœnicians who accompanied them. Mr. Hope has given a representation of a Syrian helmet, the resemblance of which to those of the modern Chinese is very great, and Colonel Martin Leake has a mutilated one of bronze, of a very similar form dug up in Greece. They have alike a high ornamented spike on their tops, that which terminates the Syrian one is a lily; this, according to Herodotus, was the ornament which the Assyrians had carved on the tops of their walking-sticks. It may be seen Pl. ii, Fig. 8.

Herodotus says further, that their casques were woven, that they carried small bucklers, with lances of a moderate length, darts and poignards, and adds, that the Paphlagonians, the Ligyans, the Malions, and the Mariandynes, were armed in the same manner.

[1] I have since learnt that it was an iron morian, such as was used in the time of the Emperor Charles Vth, and, therefore, probably lost in some of the expeditions against the Tunisian pirates.

ASSYRIAN ARMOUR.

Those who lived in the time of Xerxes, we learn from Herodotus, had helmets of brass, a short sword, a buckler, and a javelin, after the manner of the Egyptians, a pectoral made of linen, and a mace of wood headed with iron.[1]

The Chaldeans were armed in the same manner.

ARMOUR OF THE MEDES AND PERSIANS.

The military dress of the Persians, previous to the reign of Cyrus the Great, was a cuirass of leather, girt about the body with a belt of the same material.[2] Herodotus also mentions, that they wore pectorals of linen, several times folded and stitched; and from Plutarch[3] we learn, that, among the spoils taken at the battle of Issus, there was one which so much pleased Alexander the Great, that he wore it himself as part of his martial habit.

The Median dress introduced by Cyrus, superseded this more simple attire of the Persians. His soldiers were consequently adorned with a cloak, fastened with a buckle, and called Candys, the colour of which was a particularly high-prized purple,[4] and not permitted to the common people.

The Median and Persian soldiers belonging to the army of Xerxes, according to Herodotus, had each a tiara for his head that was impenetrable, a tunic, covered with plates of steel like the scales of a fish, and adorned with sleeves of various colours; an Egyptian pectoral on his breast, with the anaxyrides, or trowsers, which covered his legs and thighs, and, as we see on the Parthians, in Hope's Costumes, drawn in round the ankles. Herodotus adds, that they carried a target of cane, strongly compacted, which served as a shield, and was called *Γερρα*. This covered the quiver, in which were long arrows made of cane, and a short bow. They bore in their hands javelins, and had a sword suspended from a belt upon the right side. Some of the cavalry, however, wore helmets of brass.

In the sculptures at Persepolis[5] there are two rows of Persian soldiers wearing this tiara, which thence appears to have been cylindrical, and there is another row in helmets, which are the same hemispherical scull caps as are worn by the cavalry in Persia at this day. Each soldier of one of the rows with the tiara has a bow on his left side, placed perpendicularly, so that one end passes over his shoulder, while the other goes down to his thigh: he has a quiver at his back, and a short spear or javelin in his hand. Polyænus[6] says, that in Persia, Alexander the Great had at his court 500 Persian archers, in different dresses of yellow, blue, and scarlet, before whom stood 500 Macedonians, with silver shields. This same author tells us, that the quiver was worn at the shoulder by the Persians. The other row of the sculptures represents soldiers with the same kind of javelin, but, as Herodotus describes, the target obscures his quiver. That this target was the gerra we learn from its resemblance to that carried by Theban warriors on the Greek fictile vases, knowing as we do, that the Greeks borrowed the Gerra from the Persians. It is fiddle-shaped, and has an ornament in the centre. Both these rows are in flowing garments, but in the row, in which the figures wear the helmet, each of them has a tunic, apparently of leather, girt round the waist, as was the custom of the most antient Persians. Each carries a javelin in his hand, has a sword suspended from the belt on the right side, and on his left his bow in a half case, such as is still used. The chariots sculptured at Persepolis have a great resemblance to those of the Greeks.

[1] Several brass mace-heads, which have wooden handles fixed in them, may be seen in the British Museum.

[2] Herod. in Clio. [3] In Vit. Alex. [4] Called by Strabo *αλιπορφυρος*.

[5] See Chardin's Persepolis; Montfaucon Antiq. expliq. Vol. II, p. 402; and the sculptures now in the British Museum.

[6] Lib. iv, c. 3. [7] Lib. xiii, c. 6.

Xenophon tells us, the Persians had arms for close combat, a pectoral upon their breasts, and a shield in the left hand; and speaking of the army of Cyrus, says, many of them had handsome tunics and elegant pectorals, with helmets. Their horses for the chariots were armed with forehead-pieces, and had plates upon their flanks, so that the whole army glittered with brass, and appeared beautifully decked in scarlet robes. In another passage he tells us, that the arms of Cyrus and those of his companions, which formed a royal guard, were gilt, and differed in no one particular, excepting that his were brighter, having been more highly polished,[1] shining like a mirror. They had scarlet or purple tunics,[2] (which, as we have seen, they adopted from the Medes), a pectoral of brass, brazen helmets with white crests, swords and spears, the shafts of which were made of the cornel tree. Their horses were armed with forehead-pieces, breast-plates, and side-pieces, which last served to protect the thighs of the riders.[3] Thus we see that the brazen thorax was derived from the linen pectoral, and that this change was first effected by the Persians. From this description we further learn, that the chamfrein, as it was called in Europe, or forehead-plate for the horse,[4] the poitral, or breast-plate for that animal, and plates to protect his flanks and the thighs of his rider, such as were adopted in Europe in the fifteenth century, had all their origin in Persia. Perhaps the armour to protect the flanks of the horses, and the thighs of the riders at the same time, were something like what are still worn in Persia, in the form of large triangular projecting flaps, attached to the side-plates of the horsemen, which answer the same purpose. As these are composed of scales of iron, covered over with embroidered velvet, they seem of greater antiquity than the coat of mail worn with them.

In the time of Alexander the Great this splendour in military equipments was carried to the highest degree of extravagance. Charidemus, a Persian nobleman, observed to this monarch, that the soldiers of his country were clothed in coloured garments, and glittered in armour of gold, far exceeding in brilliancy and riches any pomp that had preceded.

Quintus Curtius, moreover, describes the manner in which Darius appeared with his army: "The guards of the Persian monarch were called immortal, because as fast as one of them died his place was filled up by another. The richness of their dress far exceeded that of any other corps, they all had torques of gold round their necks, their tunics embroidered with gold, with sleeves adorned with pearls. The sword-belt of Darius was of gold, and from it was suspended his scimitar, the scabbard of which was composed of one entire pearl."[5] The torques were a military ornament, common to many countries, and often at this day, dug up in Britain and Ireland,[6] but were derived originally from Egypt. In the earliest periods of Egyptian history, its warriors were generally ornamented with a torque and bracelets. While Joseph the Jewish patriarch, was in renown in that country, the principal men, we learn from the Pentateuch, wore רבד a wreathed necklace or torque of gold, rings, and bracelets: and Cambyses, the Persian conqueror of Egypt, sent a wreathed neck-bracelet, with bracelets for the arms, of gold, to the king of Ethiopia.[7]

Ammianus Marcellinus[8] speaks of a multitude of horses rode by the Persian cavalry, entirely

[1] *Ωσπερ κατοπτρον εξελαμπει*, are the words of the author. It is a curious fact that the four plates, viz. for the back, breast, and two sides of more modern Persian armour are called in that language Chúr-aineh, i. e. the four mirrors

[2] *Χιτωσι φοινικοις*, Phœnician tunics. The Phœnician or Tyrian dye was famous in antient times, and was produced from the shell-fish on that coast, called murex purpura.

[3] Julius Pollux, lib. I, c. 10, seems to refer to this passage.

[4] In Asia, however, it does not appear to have enveloped the horse's head like a mask, but was merely a protection for the forehead, probably, a circular plate, with a spike in the centre: and yet Julius Pollux seems to allude to coverings of gold for the ears and cheeks. Probably those used by the tribes of central Africa give a fair idea of them, as though they have coverings for the cheeks, they are merely noseguards.

[5] Quintus Curtius.

[6] Several specimens of these may be seen engraved in the Archæologia, published by the Society of Antiquaries, and in the Transactions of the Royal Irish Academy.

[7] Herodotus, Thalia.

[8] Lib. XXIV.

defended, operimentis scorteis, with leathern housings. Heliodorus[1] observes again, that the heavy armour worn by the Persian horses rendered them immoveable when they lost their conductors. The Persians called their armed steeds clibanarii. A sculpture of Chosro Puris at Tackti Bostan, represents him in armour apparently of rings, set edgewise, and his horse with his front-half entirely covered with little plates connected by chains.

The method of inlaying the blades and hilts of the scimitars with gold, still practised by the Persians, seems very antient, for when we read in Herodotus,[2] that among those taken as spoils by the Greeks, were many golden swords, we must understand the expression in this way. Plate II, Fig. 1, is the bow and quiver carried by the soldiers who wore the cap, Fig. 5. Fig. 3, the bow, bow-case, and spear, which armed the soldiers who wore the scullcap, Fig. 4, and carried the gerra, Fig. 2.

The Hyrcanians and Bactrians, according to Herodotus, were armed precisely like the Persians; and the Cissians likewise, except that, instead of tiaras, they wore mitres.

SAGARTIAN ARMS.

These were a people of Persian extraction, that accompanied Xerxes in his expedition against Greece. They are described by Herodotus, as retiarii, for he tells us, they had no other[3] weapon than a short sword, and a net made of cord, which they threw over their opponents, and when they had the good fortune to entangle them, they immediately destroyed them with their swords.[4] It is much more probable, that from this people the Greeks first heard of the retiarii, than the story of Diogenes Laertius, who says, that Pittacus, one of the seven sages of Greece, in a war between the Athenians and inhabitants of Mitylene, challenged the enemy's general to single combat, and then with a net, which he secretly brought, entangled and overcame him. The contest of the retiarii and mirmillones must, however, have been instituted some time after.

PARTHIAN ARMOUR.

Mr. Hope, Pl. XIII, of his Costume of the Antients, has given the figure of a Parthian monarch, with his bow and javelin, the former of which is made of two pieces, fitted into a handle; and the latter has a large ball at the butt-end, and a lozenge-shaped blade at the other. Justin[5] gives the following description of the Parthians, "their speech is a medium between the Scythian and Median languages, containing a mixture of both. In antient times their costume was peculiar to their country, but on their acquisition of wealth it was composed of transparent and flowing garments, like that of the Medes. Their mode of arming is a trifling deviation from that of the Scythians. Their army is not raised from freemen, as is practised by other nations, but for the most part of slaves. The power of manumission is withheld from the common class of them, and therefore their progeny are born in servitude. With equal care these and their children are taught to ride and shoot with the utmost attention. The richest persons provide the king with the greatest number of horsemen; hence, when Antony undertook his campaign against the Parthians, out of 50,000 cavalry, only 400 were freemen. They know not how to fight in close quarters, or drive away a besieging army, but they fight while their horses are in pursuit, or while in retreat, often, indeed, feigning flight, that their adversaries may incautiously be more effectually wounded. The signal is given to them in battle not by a trumpet,

1 Lib. IX, Æthiopicorum. 2 In Calliope. 3 Polymnia.

4 It is a curious fact, that Cortez met with retiarii among the Mexicans, and afterwards made some use of them.

5 Lib. XLI. His words are, Munimentum (Parthis) equisque loricæ plumatæ sunt, quæ utrumque toto corpore tegunt. They must, therefore, have greatly resembled the Dacians on the Trajan column.

Drawn by S. R. Meyrick.

Etched by R. B.

ASIATIC ARMS AND ARMOUR.

but a kettle-drum.[1] They are unable to keep up a long contest, not being capable of adding perseverance to impetuosity, indeed, in the heat of the battle they often take to flight, and from that flight renew the attack. They make no use of gold except in adorning their arms." Their horses were covered with plumated loricæ, which completely enveloped their bodies. Suidas undertakes to explain this more fully. He says, the lorica of the Parthian cavalry is after this manner, the forė part covers the breast, outside of the thighs, and external part of the hands and legs; the posterior part the back, neck, and whole of the head; but there are fibulæ at the sides with which both parts are united, and in this manner the horsemen have the appearance of being wholly covered with steel. Yet it by no means interferes with or hinders the movement of their limbs, so curiously is it manufactured, notwithstanding it fits quite close. They also arm their horses in a similar manner wholly in iron, and even to their hoofs. Plate II, Fig. 6 and 7, show the Parthian bow and javelin.

PALMYRENE ARMOUR.

Zozimus tells us, that the cavalry of Palmyra placed great confidence in their armour, which was very strong and secure, being covered with brass or iron. The Emperor Aurelianus, therefore, in order to destroy them, made his soldiers pretend to fly, which wearied their men and horses through the excessive heat and weight of their armour, when wheeling suddenly round, he charged and overthrew them, his troops treading them on the ground as they fell from their horses. As we find them called Clibanarii in the Notitia Imperii, their armour must have resembled that of the Persians.

SARACEN ARMOUR.

The Saracens, in the time of Valentinian, says Zozimus, had fleet horses, and well managed the lance, which they wielded with great strength.

ARMENIAN ARMOUR.

The helmet of the Armenians was cylindrical, with a flap hanging down behind, which was slit so as to form ear-pieces, as well as a protection for the head and shoulders. Herodotus says, they were armed like the Phrygians, from whom they were a colony. In the time of Constantius, according to Zozimus, the Armenians served as mounted archers in the Roman armies. Plate II, Fig. 9, exhibits an Armenian helmet.

INDIAN ARMOUR.

The Indians, says Herodotus,[2] who inhabit Asia, clothe themselves with garments made of rushes, which they cut from the river, and interlaying them together like mats, work them into the form of the thorax. They use bows and arrows, both made of cane, but the latter headed with iron. This military costume greatly resembles that of the antient Peruvians, and the modern inhabitants of the South Seas.

[1] Tympano, the nacaise of the modern Asiatics. The tympanum was of metal, and sometimes covered with a skin. Indeed, the drum as well as tabour was known to the antients, as Montfaucon has satisfactorily proved.

[2] Thalia.

SCYTHIAN ARMOUR.

Many of the Scythians, according to Herodotus, clothed themselves with the skins of men, as other nations did with those of beasts, and with the skins of the right hands of their enemies they made coverings[1] for their quivers. They likewise made cups of the sculls of those they had slain, a fact which is corroborated by the practice having been retained by their Gothic descendants.[2] The poorer sort, adds the historian, clothed themselves with leather to which the more wealthy added ornaments of gold. As he speaks of their quivers, they had doubtless bows, and, indeed, archery was their constant practice, war and the chase supplying frequent opportunities. Isidorus attributes this art to the progenitors of the Scythians, and we read of the Greeks, in their earliest times, sending their nobility to be instructed by this people in the art of shooting. Thus Hercules was taught by Teutarus, a Scythian swain, from whom he received a bow and arrows of that country. Hence Lycophron,[3] speaking of them, says,

Τοῖς Τἑυταρέιοις βουκολου πτερώμασὶ

"With arrows which he had from Teutarus."

Lycophron also, arms Minerva with a Mæotian bow, and, in the same place, speaks of that which Hercules bequeathed to Philoctetes, calling it a Scythian dragon. Theocritus, as well as Lycophron, particularly distinguishes between the shape of the Scythian bows and that of the Greeks, the former resembling a crescent, or the letter C.[4]

On the column of Theodosius, at Constantinople, are sculptured some arms and armour of the Scythians in his time. They consist of a tunic, apparently wadded, with a girdle and cross-belts of leather studded, the sleeves very short, but secured with two bands like the belts; a conical helmet of leather, secured with iron bands, and surmounted by a spike; an oval shield; a mace and a club, both spiked. These are copied on Plate II, Fig. 10, 11, 12, and 13.

According to Herodotus, the Sacæ, a Scythian nation, had conical helmets, bows, and arrows, according to the custom of Scythia, axes, and sagares, which, Xenophon tells us, were double-axes.

SARMATIAN ARMOUR.

A figure on Trajan's column exhibits a Sarmatian as wearing loose trowsers drawn round the ankle, and with a high cap, greatly resembling that worn at the present day by the Persians; and we learn from Pausanias what was the body-armour of that people. He saw a Sarmatian cuirass in the temple of Esculapius, suspended there as a trophy, and further informs us, that "the Sarmatians neither possess iron themselves, nor derive it by importation, as these barbarians keep themselves more than all others free from communication with foreign countries. In consequence, therefore, of the want of this metal, they have devised wicker instead of iron tops for their spears. Their bows and arrows are of cornel wood, the piles of the latter being of wicker. They likewise, in battle, throw chains about every enemy they meet, and at the same time making their horses wheel about, throw down the person thus entangled. In order to make their body-armour, they collect the hoofs of horses, and, after purifying, cut them into slices, and polish the pieces so as to resemble the scales of a dragon, or a pine cone when green. This scale-like composition they perforate and sew together with the nerves of horses and

[1] Perhaps only the caps to them. The human skin has been tried merely for experiment, and found to make most beautiful leather.

[2] To drink nectar from the sculls of their enemies, in the hall of their god Odin, was declared to be the privilege of all who fell in battle.

[3] Cassandra, v. 56.

[4] There is a figure with the Mæotian bow, on a fictile vase, in Hamilton's Etruscan Antiquities, Vol. IV, Pl. CXVI, and copied Pl. II, Fig. 14. The modern Tartar bow is of this form when unstrung, as appears by two specimens in the Asiatic armoury at Goodrich Court.

oxen, and the body-armour thus manufactured is not inferior to that of the Greeks, either in regard to elegance or strength, as it will sustain a blow given from a distance, or at close quarters."

In Mr. Gwennap's collection of armour there was a cuirass exactly answering this description and brought from some part of Asia.[1] It is composed of the hoofs of some animal, which are stitched together, supporting one another without being fastened on any under garment, and formed in perpendicular rows overlapping each other. It is figured in Plate III, Fig. 1. Ammianus confirms the account of Pausanias, by saying that the Sarmati and Quadi armed themselves with loricæ made with shavings of horn,[2] polished into the form of feathers, and sewn upon a linen tunic. In the time of Augustus Cæsar, Valerius Flaccus seems to imply, that the Sarmatians wore chain mail, and covered their horses with the same.[3] His words are,

"............ Riget his molli lorica catenâ,
Id quoque tegmen equis."

"These are confined by the lorica of yielding chain,
And such also is the covering for their horses."

Whether this poetical language does in reality designate that ingenious armour, undoubtedly of Asiatic origin, and termed double chain-mail, and how far the writer may be relied on, in attributing it to the Sarmatians, may be fairly doubted,[4] as Pausanius before, and Tacitus and Ammianus after him, assign to them the plumated or scaled species. Tacitus thus speaks, "The weapons of the Rhoxalani, a people of Sarmatia, are long spears or swords, of an enormous size, which they wield with both hands. They have neither shields nor bucklers, but their chiefs wear armour formed of small plates, or hardened hides, sewn together. Although impenetrable to the thrust, it is still a great impediment to any that have been thrown down by the charge of an enemy, preventing their being able to rise again: not having the power, therefore, to retreat, they are cut to pieces, more like men bound in fetters than soldiers armed for the field of battle." Mr. Gwennap's cuirass justifies the term "fetters." The Roman historian, nevertheless, acknowledges that their cavalry are impetuous, fierce, and irresistible in their onset, although that cannot be said of the infantry.[5]

SUSIAN ARMOUR.

Xenophon describes[6] the military dress of Abradates, king of the Susians, as consisting of a linen pectoral, a golden helmet with a crest of violet colour, arm-pieces, broad bracelets, and a purple tunic reaching to the feet.

MOSYNŒCIAN ARMOUR.

This people, we learn from Xenophon,[7] wore double tunics as a defence, with leathern helmets like those of the Paphlagonians, from the middle of which there arose a tuft of hair, braided to a point, resembling a tiara. Their shields were made in the shape of an ivy-leaf, composed of the hides of white oxen, with the hair on.

In ancient times the shape of the shield had much to do with the mythology of the people, and therefore it was circular to represent the sun, crescent-like to imitate the moon, &c. The ivy-leaf was sacred to Bacchus, and it might be from this people that the Greeks derived the pelta, which Xenophon describes as of the same form.

[1] Japan, as it has been said of late, but I am inclined to doubt it.
[2] Lib. VI.
[3] Ex cornibus rasis.
[4] See a paper on this subject in the 19th volume of the Archæologia.
[5] Tacit. Hist. Lib. 1.
[6] Lib. IV.
[7] Anabasis, Lib. V.

THRACIAN ARMOUR.

Those Thracians who accompanied Xerxes into Greece covered their heads with a cap or helmet made of foxes' skins, and their bodies with a tunic, and mantle of various colours: their shoes were bound above their ankles, and they carried small bucklers in the form of a half-moon; every one had a javelin and a short dagger.[1] The Thracians, who retained their original name in Asia, came into the field with small bucklers composed of untanned hides, two Lycian javelins for each man, with a helmet of brass, having ears and horns like an ox, of the same metal; and their legs were covered with Phœnician cloth.[2] These helmets were worn also by the Phrygians, though but rarely, they were, however, adopted by the Greeks, and, according to Diodorus Siculus, by the Belgic Gauls. Being formed as typical of the religion of the country, the horns of the ox or cow being emblematic of the moon, they were a fit accompaniment for the crescent-like shields. Plate iii, Fig. 19, exhibits a Thracian helmet; and Fig. 20, a Thracian shield, impressed with the representation of a serpent, the symbol of the sun.

From Roman sculptures,[3] made by the Thracian cohorts in the service of that empire, we find them armed with a curious kind of javelin or lance, the shaft of which appears composed of little bands, perhaps of cane, and becoming larger towords the head, where it terminates in a round ball, on this is affixed either a pyramidal-shaped spear-head, or a short or long spike. Plate iii, Fig. 4 and 5, are these Thracian weapons; Fig. 6, a Mysian one; and Fig. 7, a Macedonian; all having some resemblance to each other. Fig. 3, is the Mysian shield, which was used with Fig. 6, and seen inside, to shew that it was held by the hand, and not put on the arm. A weapon, much resembling the strange one above noticed, Fig. 4, is still used in part of the Persian dominions.[4]

The retiarii of the Roman games were generally Thracians,[5] and these were matched with the mirmillones, or secutores. They bore in their left hands a three pointed lance, called a trident, and a dagger, and in their right a net, by which they tried to entangle their adversary, and then with the dagger to despatch him: if they missed their aim they protected themselves with the trident, and then instantly took to flight to prepare for a second cast of the net. Juvenal[6] thus alludes to this practice,

> "............... movet ecce tridentem,
> Postquam vibrata pendentia retia dextra,
> Nequicquam effudit."

> "............... Lo! he moves his trident,
> Having, thrown without effect the hanging nets,
> Brandishing his right hand."

But the antagonist as swiftly pursuing to prevent this design taking effect, was called a secutor or pursuer.

The retiarii were clad in a short tunic, or cuirass, which came up to their breasts, and reached nearly half way of their thighs, their left arms were protected by padded linen twisted round them, out of which issued a shoulder-shield high enough to guard the face. This shoulder-shield was called galerus, as we are told by the Scholiast on Juvenal, who says it was thus affixed to the shoulder, to leave the hands free for the management of the net. It was of different shapes, in the marble dug up at Chester, and in the tessellated pavement, both engraved in the Vetusta Monumenta, published by the Society of Antiquaries of London, it is square; on a lamp, engraved by Montfaucon, Vol. V, Pl. cxcvi, curved at top like the thureos; and in the pavement at Bignor, in Sussex, where the figures are in colours, semicircular. From the representation on the lamp, it appears that the Thracians fought sometimes on their knees.

The arms of the secutores were a helmet, a shield, and a sword or leaden mace.

[1] Herod. in Polymnia. [2] Ibid. [3] See Montfaucon's Antiq. expl.

[4] One in the Asiatic Armoury at Goodrich Court has its blade made to cut and thrust.

[5] Cic. Phil. vii, 6; Liv. xli, 20. Horat. Sat. ii, 6, 44. Suet. Calig. 32. Juv. viii, 201. Auson. in Monosyll. 102.

[6] Sat. viii, v. 203.

Plate III.

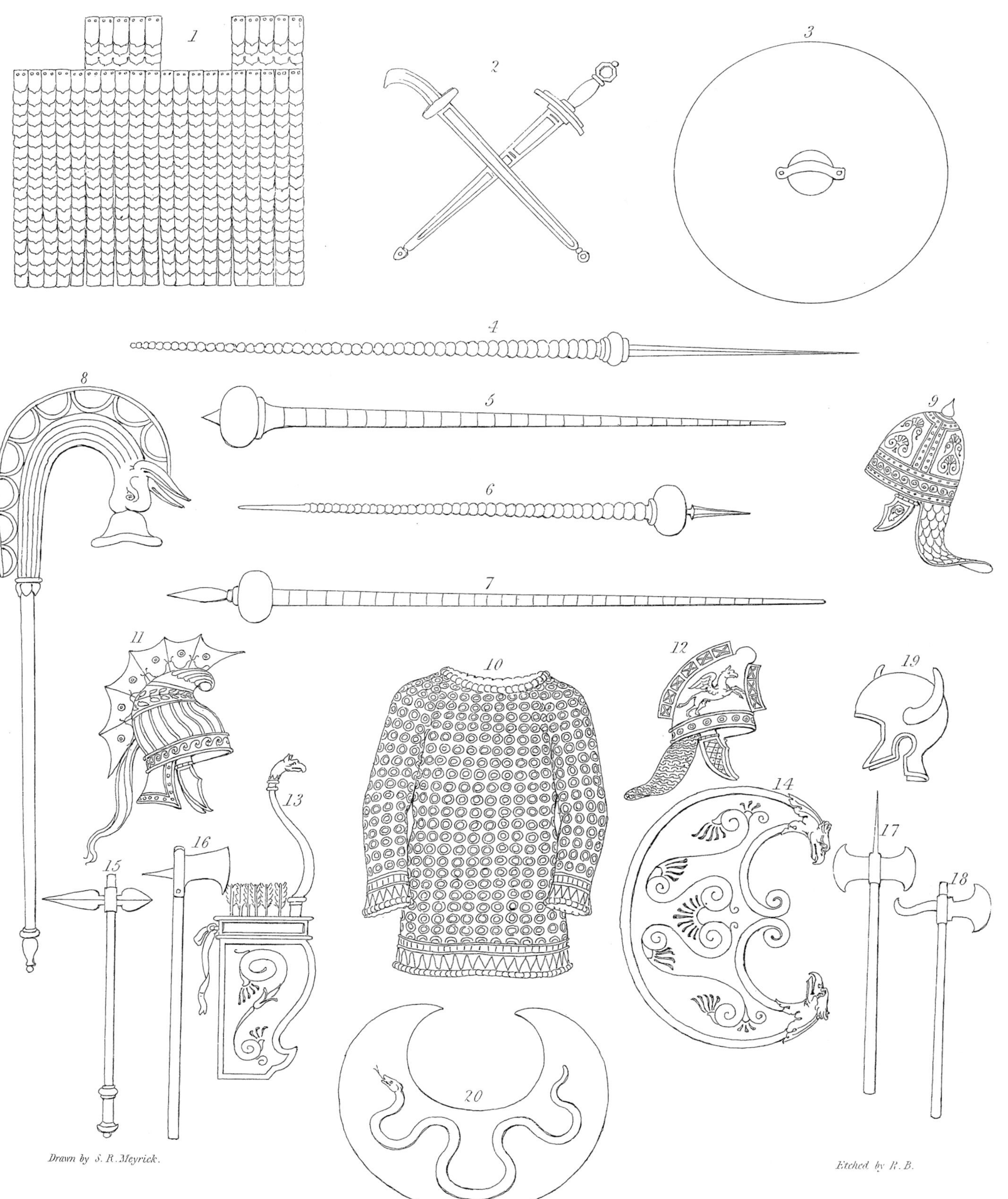

ASIATIC ARMS AND ARMOUR.

DACIAN ARMOUR.

In the early periods of the Dacian history, their warriors were habited very much after the Phrygian manner, and the large Cossack trowsers were common to them and the Sarmatians. They wore the Phrygian bonnet, but their helmets were high scullcaps, differently shaped from the Phrygian, with a spike at top, moveable cheek-pieces, and a flap of scale-work to cover the neck. On the Trajan column not only many of the Dacian soldiers themselves, but several of their horses, appear entirely enveloped in a covering of small scales, in close contact with the body and limbs: they are armed with bows and arrows, and a sword of the sickle kind, having its edge on the inner curve.[1]

Herodotus says, the Dacians, Parthians, Chorasmians, Sogdians, Gandarians, and Arians, were all armed in the time of Xerxes like the Bactrians, except that the bows of the last resembled those of the Medes. He farther tells us, that the Pactyes, the Uians, the Myces, and the Paricanians, all carried bows, that the Sarangi had bows and pikes like those of the Medes, and that the Caspians had bows of cane which grew in their country, and swords. In Plate iii, Fig. 2, the uppermost sword is that of a Dacian soldier, and the under one, such as used in the Isle of Cos, very closely resembling those of the Thracians. Fig. 8, is a Dacian standard, representing the serpent, an object of Pagan worship, and terminating in what appears to have been a bell. Fig. 9, a Dacian helmet, its similarity to the scullcaps so generally worn in Asia at the present time must be obvious.

SASPIRIAN ARMOUR.

Those of this nation who were in the army of Xerxes, Herodotus tell us, had helmets of wood. The Allarodians were armed in the same manner.

COLCHIAN ARMOUR.

Like the Saspirians, wooden helmets were the distinguishing armour of this nation when under the command of Xerxes.

MYSIAN ARMOUR.

These people, according to Herodotus, wore a casque, had little bucklers, and used javelins hardened at their ends with fire. It has been already observed, that Plate iii, Fig. 3 and 6, exhibit a Mysian shield and javelin, such as were used in the time of the Romans.

LYCIAN ARMOUR.

The Lycians had a covering of goat-skins upon their shoulders, they wore pectorals upon their breasts, and their legs were defended with greaves: they had also caps adorned with crests, stuck round with feathers.[2] On the column of Trajan some of the warriors appear with caps of this kind, and they have been supposed to be Moors of Africa, but whether the Lycians preserved this fashion to so late a period we have no means to determine. Every one of the Lycians, Herodotus further informs us,[3] carried a bow of cornel, with arrows of cane unfledged, a dart, a faulchion, and a short sword.

The Milyans, according to the same author, carried short lances, or had Lycian bows; their helmets were of skins. The Moschi had wooden helmets, little bucklers, short darts, but long lances. The Tibarenians and the Macroni were armed like the Moschi. The Mares had woven casques, little bucklers of leather, and darts.

[1] Similar to these were the seaxes of the Saxons, and such are still used by the Albanians of Turkey, several varieties of which are in the Asiatic Armoury at Goodrich Court.

[2] Πιλους πτεριοσι περιεστεφανωμένους.

[3] Polymnia.

PHRYGIAN ARMOUR.

The prevailing helmet of the Asiatics, bordering on the Euxine and the Archipelago, appears to have been that which is generally known by the name of the Phrygian, and of which the characteristic features are, its point at top being bent down forward, and its long flaps descending on the shoulders: it was of leather or metal, and enriched with embossed ornaments. To many the flaps appear four in number, and probably were cut out of the legs of the animals whose hide or skin formed the body of the casque.[1] In the figures of the Amazons, which may be considered as fabulous representations of the inhabitants of Asia Minor, bordering on the Phrygians, we often see the beak of the helmet terminate in the bill of a griffin, and on the spine or back of the casque rise the jagged crest of that fabulous animal. Minerva appears on fictile vases, sometimes in a Phrygian helmet of this species, probably as she was worshipped at Troy; and Roma on many Latin coins also wears it, in order, no doubt, to indicate the kindred which the Romans claimed with the Trojans. Mr. Hope has represented one Phrygian helmet, the neck flap of which is composed of double chain mail, or interlaced rings.[2] I cannot help regretting that he has not given his authority for this, as, if correct, it is the oldest specimen extant, and excites our surprise that such an ingenious contrivance should not have been copied before the 13th century.[3] The body-armour of the Phrygians was a tunic, with tight sleeves reaching to the wrists, and covered with flat rings, as appears from a bronze in the possession of I. Hawkins, Esq., of Bignor Park, Sussex.

The chief defensive weapon was the lunated shield, with a rise in the centre of the crescent, and the offensive ones were the bipennis, or double-bladed axe, the club, and the bow and arrow, generally carried in two different partitions of the same quiver.

Many of the Asiatic nations were celebrated for their constant use and skilful management of horses, and are often represented as fighting on horseback against the Greeks on foot. In Plate III, Fig. 11 and 12, are Phrygian helmets. Fig. 10, a tunic of flat contiguous rings. Fig. 13, the quiver, bows, and arrows. Fig. 14, the shield. And Fig. 15, 16, 17, and 18, Phrygian battle-axes.[4] Among the paintings found at Herculaneum is a Phrygian archer in his proper costume and colours.

CARIAN ARMOUR.

Those Carians who arrived in Egypt in the reign of Psammetichus appeared in brazen armour.[5] We further learn, from Herodotus, that they were the first who added crests to their helmets, and ornaments to their shields. They were the first, too, who gave the shield its handle. Before their time such as bore shields had no other means of managing them but by a piece of leather, suspended from the neck over the left shoulder.[6] Alluding to their addition to the helmet, Alcæus says,

Λόφον τε σέιων Καρικὸν.
"Shaking his Carian crest."

They were the first who served for pay, which was at that time reckoned so great a mark of servility, that, Strabo informs us, they rendered their name infamous.

[1] In imitation of this the hoods of mail attached to the modern Asiatic scullcaps terminate in four vandykes, or pointed pieces.

[2] This, with the expression of Valerius Flaccus, "molli lorica catenâ," seems to imply that the chain-mail was in reality known to the antients. It may be seen Pl. III, Fig. 12.

[3] On an application to that gentleman I find that, as his authority is not now discoverable, it is probably an error of his engraver. See a paper of mine, on the lorica catenâ, in the 19th vol. of the Archæologia.

[4] A Phrygian gladiator on a Roman lamp, with an oblong shield, may be seen in Monfaucon's Antiq. expl. Vol. V, Pl. CXCVI.

[5] Herod. in Euterpe. [6] Ibid. Clio; and Strabo, Lib. XIV.

IONIANS.

These, like the Carians at the same period, wore brazen armour.[1]

LYDIANS.

The Lydians, Herodotus tells us, were armed just like the Greeks.

CILICIANS.

The Cilicians had casques according to the fashion of their country, small bucklers of untanned ox-hide, swords like the Egyptians, and each carried two javelins in the time of Xerxes.

PAMPHYLIANS.

The Pamphylians, says Herodotus, were armed in the Grecian manner.

ÆOLIANS.

These were armed like the Greeks, as were also the Peloponnesians.

CYPRIANS.

Those of Cyprus, according to Herodotus, were armed like the Greeks.

GRECIAN ARMOUR.

The Grecians had their share of military glory in an eminent degree, and of these the Lacedemonians were considered as the most warlike. They were soldiers by profession, the laws of their country laying them under that obligation; they were accustomed from their childhood to undergo the severest trials both of fatigue and danger, and taught to be always prepared to live or die as emergencies required.

Οι δὲ θάνον, οὐ ζῆν θέμενοι καλὸν οὐδὲ τὸ θνήσκειν,
Αλλὰ τὸ ταῦτα καλῶς ἀμφότερ ἐκτελέσαι.[2]

"They died, not giving the preference to life or death,
But, as valour required, were prepared for both."

Next to the Lacedemonians the Athenians were considered the best troops, and there are not wanting instances in which they disputed the Spartan superiority. The Grecian soldiers, before the age of Pericles, maintained themselves at their own expence, and for fear they should desert were marked with characters punctured on their hands, *στίγματα ἐν ταῖς χερσὶ*.[3] The profession of a soldier, as in all primitive nations, was rendered more honourable by being confined to free citizens, slaves never being permitted to bear arms except in cases of the most extreme danger.

The Grecian armies were composed of various sorts of soldiers, the principal part were infantry, but they had cavalry, some who fought in chariots and some on elephants. The foot soldiers were distinguished by the terms *ὁπλιται*, "those who wore armour," and carried broad shields and long spears: and *ψιλοὶ*, the light troops, who, with no other protection than a helmet, were armed with darts, bows and arrows, or slings. The *πέλτασται*, who carried the *πέλτα*, or narrow-pointed shield,[4] and spears, though a species of light troops, were considered as an intermediate kind. The heavy-armed foot were at all times the strength of the Grecian armies.

[1] Ὁπλισθέντας χαλκῳ. [2] Plutarch. Pelopida. [3] Ælian's Tactics.

[4] The companion of Ajax is represented as one of those on a vase in Sir William Hamilton's Etruscan Antiquities, Vol. III. Pl. lvii. Xenophon says, the πέλτα was in the form of an ivy-leaf and first used by the Amazons.

The light-armed troops were formed of the poorer citizens, hence they do not appear in the sculptured frieze of the Parthenon; their mode of fighting was desultory, and having thrown their weapons, they frequently retired behind the protecting shields[1] of the heavy-armed infantry. As was the case with our Norman ancestors, the cavalry of the Grecians was composed of such only as were possessed of estates, which enabled them to provide horses at their own charge: those, therefore, were not very numerous. Their horses had bridles, with bits called *λύκοι*, from their resemblance to the teeth of wolves, which, from being jagged,[2] rendered them very powerful; and though on the Elgin marbles there is no appearance of saddles, the *ἐφίππια*, or horse-coverings, made of cloth, leather or the skins of wild beasts, were certainly used at a later period. According to Julius Pollux,[3] the Greeks taught their horses to stoop when they wanted to mount them. The chariots were probably used only by the nobles, being richly embossed with gold and silver ornaments. Thus Homer,

> Ἅρμα δέ οι χρυσῷ τε καὶ ἀργύρῳ εὖ ἤσκηται.[4]
>
> "Silver and gold his chariot did adorn."

And again,

> Ἄρματά τε χρυσῷ πεπυκασμένα, κασσιτέρῳτε.[5]
>
> "Chariots richly adorned with gold and tin."

They were likewise furnished with curious hangings:

> ἀμφὶ δὲ πέπλοι
> Πέπταντας.[6]
>
> " . . . . Round about hangings
> Expanded wide."

These hangings do not appear on the sculptured frieze of the Parthenon, the chariots there are about sixteen inches above the ground, with two wheels each, having four spokes. They are mounted from behind, being there open; but on the sides and in front enclosed; these sides are furnished with handles, very conveniently placed for those who would get up into them. The chariots, mentioned by Homer, are for the most part drawn by two horses abreast:

> . . . . . παρὰ δὲ σφιν ἑκάστῳ διζυγες ἵπποι
> Ἕστασαν.[7]
>
> " . . . . . To every chariot two yoked horses
> Stand."

To these a third was sometimes added, but not like the other two, which were fastened to the pole; he ran by the side, attached only by traces. They were sometimes drawn by four, as when Hector, in the Iliad, calls to his four harnessed steeds; and Homer, in another place, says:

> . . . . . ὡς ἐν πεδίῳ τετράορες ἵπποι.[8]
>
> " . . . . . As in the field the four reined steeds."

On the Elgin marbles they appear sometimes drawn by two, sometimes by three, sometimes by four horses. Every chariot carried two men, whence it was termed *δίφρος*, and this occurs perpetually in the Elgin marbles. One of these holds the reins, and we find he was thence called *ἡνίοχος*; and although this office was sometimes performed by persons of quality, it was considered as inferior to that of the *παραβάτης*, or warrior, who commanded him where to drive. These warriors, on the frieze before mentioned, and which is referred to as of fixed date,[9] are all heavy armed, that is, they have

1 Iliad, θ. v. 266.
2 Such have been dug up in Italy, and several are preserved at Goodrich Court.
3 Lib. I, c. ix.
4 Iliad, κ.
5 Iliad, ύ.
6 Iliad, έ.
7 Iliad, έ.
8 Odyss. ν'.
9 The time of Pericles. See the originals in the British Museum.

on a leathern cuirass, much resembling that worn by the Roman generals,[1] and a helmet, and are armed with a spear and large circular shield. When the chariots were driven close to the enemy, the warriors frequently

. . . . ἐυπλεκέων δίφρων θόρον αἶψ' ἐπὶ γαῖαν[2]

" . . . . Leapt from their chariots on the ground"—

and when weary from the weight of their armour, retired into their chariots, and thence annoyed their enemies with darts and missile weapons. The chariots, however, on the Elgin marbles are not furnished with these latter, like those of the Græco-Egyptians, sculptured on the walls of the tombs of the kings at Thebes. It is said, that the Greeks in very antient times had chariots, δρεπανοφόροι, armed with scythes, but I have never met with any in antient sculpture, and they were contemned in the better days of Greece as inconvenient, and not likely, when used by an enemy, to do them much damage: indeed, the chariot altogether became disused long before the time of Dionysius of Halicarnassus, though continued in his days by the Romans; and the Greeks gave their attention more fully to their cavalry.

Philomænes, the master of the Achæan horse, according to Plutarch,[3] corrected the errors in the cavalry. "He obliged them to carry a shield which, from its lightness, could be more expeditiously managed, and not wider than absolutely necessary to cover their bodies; to use lances considerably shorter than the usual sarissæ, and which, by being lighter, might be thrown at the enemy while at a distance, and yet sufficiently strong for close fight. He therefore induced them to adopt, instead of the long shield and lance, the round one with the sarissa, so that being at the same time protected with helmets, cuirasses, and greaves, they might either skirmish as light cavalry, or sustain a charge as heavy horse."

Philopœmen in like manner, according to Pausanias, changed the armour of the infantry under his command, for previous to this they used small spears, and oblong shields like the Celtic thureos, or the Persian gerra, but he persuaded them to cover their bodies with thoraxes, and their legs with greaves, and to use Argolic shields and long spears.

Greece being, however, in general hilly, will account for the preference at first given to foot soldiers for the main body of its armies; but when the Spartans carried their arms into other countries the want of cavalry was sensibly felt. Thessaly, of all the Grecian states, produced most horses, and hence they had a superiority of cavalry; but the Spartans procured theirs from the neighbouring town of Sciros, the inhabitants of which claimed, as their proper post, the left wing of the Lacedemonian armies.[4]

Of the Greek cavalry, some were ἱπποτοξόταί, or mounted archers, some ἀκροβολισται, or mounted slingers, both which may be considered as light cavalry: while the heavy horse were distinguished into regiments by their armour, as δορατοφόρόι, lancers, ξυστοφόροι, armed with sabres, κοντοφόροι, bearers of the contus,[5] θυρεοφόροι, armed with thureos, and ὑπακοντισταὶ, javelin-men. Some of those who fought on horseback had a spare horse, which they led, to supply the place of that which might be fatigued or killed; they were thence called ἀμφιπποι, and ἱππαγωγοὶ.

[1] Pausanias says, "In one of the pictures of Polygnotus there is painted, on an altar, a brazen cuirass. At present the shape of such cuirasses is very rare, but they were used in former times. It consists of two pieces of brass, one of which covers the breast and abdomen, the other the back: the interior part they call gualon, and the hinder prosegon. It appears to be a sufficient protection for the body without a shield. On this account Homer so represents the Phrygian Phorcys, because he used a gualothorax. In the temple of the Ephesian Diana, Caliphon, the Samian, has painted certain women adapting the parts of such a cuirass to Patroclus." Such a cuirass may be seen on a vase in Hamilton's Etruscan Antiquities. Vol. I. Pl. LV.

[2] Hesiod. Scuto.

[3] In Vitâ.

[4] Xenophon Cyropæd. Lib. IV; Thucydides, Lib. V.

[5] The contus was a long stout pike, used generally by sailors.

There was also a species of troops introduced by Alexander the Great, who, from being heavy armed, could dismount, give their horses to their attendants, and fight with the infantry, they were thence known by the name of *διμάχοι*.[1] The *κατάφρακτοι*, or heavy-armed horse, in later times had their horses protected by armour, made of little plates, sometimes in the shape of scales, and sometimes as flat rings placed contiguously: these were at first of brass, and then of other metals, and the armour made of them took its name from the part it covered, being called *προμετωπιδια*, frontlets;[2] *παρώτια*, ear-pieces; *παρήϊα*, cheek-coverings; *προστερνιδια*, chest-pieces; *παραπλευρίδια*, side-pieces: *παραμηρίδια*, thigh-pieces; *παρακνημίδια*, leg-pieces, &c. This custom they probably derived from the Asiatics. Elephants have been mentioned, but these were first introduced by Alexander the Great, the tractability of these animals, however, being out-weighed by their ungovernable fury when wounded, soon occasioned their disuse.

The arms of the Greeks, in Homer's time, were of bronze, as indeed with many primitive nations, copper and tin, for such was the composition, being more easily fused than iron. Tin was sometimes used by itself, thus the greaves of Achilles, the breastplate of Agamemnon, and the shield of Æneas, were composed of this metal;[3] and gold and silver formed the ornaments of armour. The armour of the early Greeks was not much, its increase was borrowed from the Asiatics;[4] after this we find it very various. The helmet was called *περικεφαλαία*, when it enveloped the whole head, such as those in the British Museum, and leaving only an opening for the sight and breath; *κράνος* when a mere scullcap, and *κόρυς*. This, as in the case of those in the British Museum,[5] was generally of brass; hence, Homer says,

> . . . . *ἀυτὰρ ἐπὶ στεφανην κεφάληφιν ἀέιρας*
> Θήκατο χαλκέιην.
>
> "... . But upon the stephane,[6] the moveable headpiece,
> He placed of brass."

In the very early periods they had been composed of skins of quadrupeds, of which none were more common than the dog, because that animal was more readily procured, though Eustathius tells us, it was *ποτάμος κύων*, a water dog, perhaps the otter: hence we have *κυνέη*, the dog's-skin helmet; *ἰκτιδεη*, that of weasel's skin; *ταυρέιη*, the bull's-hide helmet; *ἀλωπεκέη*, the fox-skin; *λεοντεη αἰγείη*, that covered with the lion's skin: but these in later times all became poetic appellations of the helmet, though made of brass. These skins were always worn with the hair on; and to render their appearance more terrible, the teeth of the animal were frequently placed grinning on their enemies, a custom that had been retained by the Mexicans. The *περικεφαλὴ* was slit up the front, in order to leave a covering for the nose, and openings for the eyes, which occasioned this part to be called *Αυλωπις* from *ωψ*, the sight; and when thrown back so as to uncover the face, necessarily left a great space between its own crown and the scull of the wearer, and generally had, in order to protect the cheeks, two leather flaps, which, when not used, were tucked up inwards. There are two in the British Museum, figured by Strutt and Grose. The *κράνος* merely covered the back part of the head, but was furnished with cheek-pieces,[7] called *ὀχους*, which tied under the chin, and were concave metal plates suspended from hinges, which, when not wanted, turned up outwards. The *κόρυς* had either a frontlet

[1] Pollux, Lib. I, cap x. One of the attendants is engraved in Hope's costume, Pl. LXXXI.

[2] A beautiful frontlet of bronze ornamented with rams' heads, &c. and reaching from between the ears to the nose of the horse, about a hand's breadth, was in the possession of the Chevalier Brönsted, chargé d'affaires from the King of Denmark to the Court of Rome. Hinges appear on each side where it would have buckled round the jaws.

[3] Iliad, ι and ν'.

[4] Euripidis Scholiastes.

[5] See the engraving of them in Grose's Antient Armour.

[6] See this explained, p. xxii.

[7] This may be seen in Ham. Etrus. Antiq. Vol. III, Pl. LVII, before cited. These sometimes hung loose and a leather strap within held the helmet in its place.

termed *ὀφρύες*, or a projecting piece, over the brow, called by the metaphorical term *γεῖσον*, the pent house.[1] There were also the *πήληξ* and the *κυνέη*. The first of these helmets was worn by the heavy-armed forces; the second by the light troops, whether cavalry or infantry; and the third by the heavy horse. The *κόρυς* was the most splendidly ornamented of any, quadrigæ, sphinxes, griffins,[2] sea-horses, and other insignia, richly embossed, often covered the surface; the *περικεφαλή* had a ridge, on which was a quantity of horse-hair from the mane, cut square at the edges; the *κρανος* sometimes had a cock's feather stuck on each side,[3] but the *κορυς* had feathers, ridges, and horse-hair of mane and tail; the ridge was called *λόφος*, the horse-hair ornament *φαλος*.[4] Homer speaks of a golden crest:

Τούξε δε οἱ κορυθα βριαρὴν κροτάφοις ἀραρῦιαν
Καλὴν, δαιδαλέην, ἐπὶ δε χρύσεον λόφον ἧκε.

"But the strong helmet on his temples, well adapted,
Beautiful, variegated, and surmounted by a golden ridge, he placed."

And that by *λόφον* he meant the ridge and not hair we learn from another passage, when speaking of this same helmet, which Vulcan made for Achilles, he adds the expression *εθειραι χρυσεαι*, golden hair, which perhaps was composed of wires of gold instead of hair, or of hair gilt.

A helmet is said by Homer to have been given by Meriones to Ulysses, strengthened within with many thongs strongly interwoven, and ornamented profusely without, with boar's teeth, quite white, and placed in curious order; in the middle was inserted a pileus, or cap of wool, to answer the purpose, probably, of a lining.

The ridge was composed of various metals, but generally such as were conceived ornamental to the helmet, and the crest was adorned with divers sorts of paint, whence Pollux gives it the epithets of *ἐυανθὴς ὑακινθινοβαφης*.[5] This crest was formed of the manes of the horses, which will account for so many in the Elgin marbles appearing hog-maned; at the bottom was sometimes added the tail of the horse, whence we read of *λόφος ἱπποχαίτης*, *κόρυς ἱπποδάσεια*, *ἵππουρις*, and on each side the crest were sometimes feathers.[6] Plumes of feathers in after ages often supplied the place of hair, and this seems to have been occasioned by Alexander the Great, who, we are told,[7] at the battle of the Granicus, was remarkable for a large plume of white feathers on his helmet. This same author tells us, that the helmet of Alexander was of steel, polished as bright as silver, and made by Theophilus; he adds that to it was affixed a gorget of the same metal set with precious stones. The common soldiers had only small crests; the chieftains were distinguished by plumes of a larger size, and frequently took a pride in wearing two, three, or four crests together. Sometimes the hair was gilt, hence, Homer says,[8]

. . . . . ἥδ' ἀστηρ ὣς ἀπελαμπεν
Ιππουρις τρυφάλεια, περισσέιοντο δ' ἔθειραι
Χρύσεαι, ἃς Ηφαιστος ἵει λόφον ἀμφὶ θαμειάς.

". . . . . Like a star, so shone around
The horse-haired helmet, having round its summit hair
Gilded, which Vulcan had placed about the ridge."

Thus we find the helmet was called, when surmounted with crests, *αμφιφαλος*, when with three, *τρυφάλεια*, and when with four *τετράφαλος*. So Apollonius,[9]

1 In European armour termed umbril. This frontlet was often not moveable but merely embossed.

2 Pliny, Lib. X. c. 49. tells us that Phidias was the first to use a griffin to embellish a helmet, on his favourite statue of Minerva in Athens.

3 Two soldiers wearing them may be seen on a lamp in Montf. Antiq. expl. Vol. V, Pl. CXCVI, which further shews the practice of a front rank kneeling being far earlier than the use of fire-arms. See further in the account of the Romans.

4 Suidas justly makes this distinction, though others have supposed no difference between them.

5 Lib. I, cap. X.

6 See Hope's Costume of the Antients, Pl. LXXV, CLXXXVII, &c.

7 Plut. in Vit. Alex.

8 Iliad, τ'. v. 382.

9 Lib. III.

Τετράφαλος φοίνικει λόφῳ ἐπελάμπετο πήληξ.

"With a four-fold crest to the Phœnician ridge dazzled the helmet."

The design is said to have been to strike terror into their enemies.[1] For the same reason Pyrrhus, king of Epirus, besides a lofty crest, had goat's-horns upon his helmet. We are told by Suidas, that the *τρίχωσις*, or crest itself, was called sometimes *κέρας*, and cows' as well as goats' horns seem to have been worn by some of the Greeks; many of them are observable in Hope's Costume of the Antients,[2] and were probably adopted from their Mythology. Other sorts of ornaments were used, as on that called *στεφάνη*, which name signifies the ridge of a mountain, and on that account is applied to helmets, having several *ἐξοχαὶ*, eminences, such as may be seen in Hope's Costume.[3] But of all the Grecian helmets, the Bœotian is said to have been the best.[4] The Macedonians had a peculiar one, termed *καυσίη*, which was composed of hides, and served instead of a cap to defend them from cold; it appears to have resembled the petasus, being broad brimmed.[5] A leathern scullcap, without any ridge or crest, Homer[6] speaks of as having been worn by Diomede:

...... ἀμφὶ δε οἱ κυνίην κεφαλῆφιν ἔθηκε
Ταυρέιην, ἄφαλόν τε, κὰι ἄλοφον, ἥ τε καταιτυξ
Κεκληται

"........ His helmet on his head he placed
Of bull's-skin, without crest, without ridge, kataityx
Called."

A small bronze antique bust of him in my possession, represents it as slit open at the ears, and terminating in thongs to tie under the chin.[7]

The Greeks often raised a trophy of arms taken from an enemy and crowned it with a single helmet, on which they inscribed the occasion of its erection. One of this kind was found at Olympia and presented to His Majesty George IV. who sent it to be deposited in the British Museum. It is of the kind termed *κράνος*, being merely a scull-cap which rises to a ridge in the centre, and has a rim about three-quarters of an inch in breadth, that has been damaged a little on one side. There is no distinction between the back and front of the helmet, nor does the shape occur in any representation of Greek warriors, with the exception of a Plate in Hope's Costume. It is so large that, although above five hundred persons have tried it on, no head has been found of sufficient size to wear it. The length of it independant of the rim is nine inches, the breadth eight, and the height seven and a half. It is made of bell metal and of rather slight substance. The inscription upon it has puzzled the learned notwithstanding its being very distinctly written. It is

ΗΙΑRΟΝΟΔΕΙΝΟΜΕΝΟΣ
ΚΑΙΤΟΙΣVRΑΚΟΣΙΟΙ
ΤΟΙΔΙΤVRΑΝΑΠΟΚVΜΑΣ

that is, substituting for the Roman letters R and V, the Greek P and Y,

ΗΙΑΡΟΝ Ο ΔΕΙΝΟΜΕΝΟΣ
ΚΑΙ ΤΟΙ ΣΥΡΑΚΟΣΙΟΙ
ΤΟΙ ΔΙ. ΤΥΡΑΝ. ΑΠΟ ΚΥΜΑΣ

1 Homer, Iliad III. So likewise Polybius, Lib. VI, in Castrametatione, says, "Besides all these they were adorned on the top with a plume and three feathers placed erect, of purple or black, almost a cubit in length, which, when other ornaments were added, made a man appear twice his natural height; very handsome indeed, but terrible to his enemies."

2 See Pl. CXXX. 3 Pl. LXXXVI. 4 Pollux, Lib. I, cap. X.

5 The petasus is frequently sculptured in the Elgin marbles. Indeed, those on the lamp in Montf. Antiq. expl. Vol. V, Pl CXCVI, are of this kind, and probably the *καυσίη*.

6 Iliad, κ.

7 A similar, but larger one, in the possession of R. P. Knight, Esq., has been engraved in Strutt's Dress and Habits of the People of England.

The person alluded to may be Hiero of Syracuse. There were two kings of Syracuse of this name, the first obtained three prizes at the Olympic games. This helmet, however, can hardly have any reference to that, as no military trophies were erected to the victory of the chariot race. We have heard of no victory obtained there by him; and Plutarch informs us that Themistocles wished to prevent his horses running, because he had refused to join against the common enemy.

In the earliest ages of Greece the warriors prided themselves on wearing the skins of the wild beasts which they had slain, at once the mark of their prowess and a tolerable protection to their bodies. Instances of this kind are to be met with in most of the antient poets, but Theocritus has described in what manner they were put on:

Αὐτὰρ ὑπὲρ νώτοιο καὶ αὐχένος ἠωρεῖτο
Ακρων δέρμα λέοντος ἀφημμένον ἐκ ποδεώνων.

"But o'er his neck and back was thrown
A lion's skin, held up by its feet."

But they afterwards adopted armour of a less dubious nature, confining it to the heavy-armed troops, both cavalry and infantry: it consisted of a band for the abdomen, named *μίτρη*, a chest-piece, called *θώραξ*, and a girdle, *ζωστηρ*, to which was attached a petticoat, called *ζῶμα*. The first was padded with wool, covered either with flat rings, or square pieces of brass,[1] and fastened at the sides: in this state it was cut round at the loins, but in the times of Homer and Pericles the *θώραξ στάδιος*, or *ςτατὸς*, so called because when taken off, it could stand upright upon its lower edge, followed the line of the abdomen, and was probably of leather, without metal plates.[2] Sometimes in front of the *μίτρη* was placed another breastpiece,[3] but this only when the thorax did not wholly cover the chest. The thorax varied in its form, at one time as a gorget it entirely covered the chest, folding over the upper part of the *μίτρη*, and covering each shoulder-blade behind;[4] at another it covered the upper part of the back, and passing over both shoulders, on the tops of which were two hinges, terminated below each breast;[5] and sometimes it covered the upper part of the back and the whole of the chest.[6] The middle part was called *γύαλον*, and the extreme part *πτέρυγες*,[7] and these were either fastened by a cord from each to a ring below,[8] or put on a kind of button.[9] The complete thorax was the most antient, and borrowed from the Persians or Egyptians; but the *ημιθωράκιον*, or half thorax, Pollux tells us, was invented by Jason. Alexander esteemed it most soldier-like, and, according to Polyænus,[10] considering the entire thorax might be a temptation to his troops to turn their backs upon their enemies, commanded them to use instead the half thorax, which, though it covered the chest, was open between the shoulder-blades. Sometimes, though rarely, the most antient thoraces of linen were worn, which were of several folds and padded. Pausanias says, he saw one of these in the temple of Grynæus Apollo, as well as in others. These, he observes, are not so useful to warriors, because they are pervious to the vehement percussions of iron. Homer[11] gives one to Ajax, son of Oileus:

1 See Hope's Costume, Pl. XLVI. CII.

2 This kind of cuirass may be seen in Hamilton's Etruscan Antiquities, Vol. I, Pl. LV. This large cuirass consisted of breast and back pieces each termed *γύαλα*, attached by pins and hooks.

3 See Hope's Costume, Pl. CII.

4 Ibid. Pl. LXXV.

5 Ibid. Pl. LXXXIV.

6 Ibid. Pl. LXX. But these distinctions may be easily seen in the Etruscan Armour, Pl. IV, of this work.

7 Pollux; Pausanias' Atticis.

8 See Hope's Costume, Pl. CII. There were two *γύαλα*, one of which may be considered as the dorsal which covered the shoulder-blades, the other the pectoral, and these were held together by means of the *περόναι* which were fastened to hinges as before mentioned. Over these *περόναι* were sometimes placed very beautiful ornaments in high relief of bronze; and those of Siris, supposed to have belonged to the armour of Pyrrhus are to be seen in the British Museum, most exquisite specimens of art and well worthy of minute examination.

9 Pausanias' Atticis.

10 Strateg. Lib. IV, c. iii.

11 Iliad, *β'*.

. . . . ὀλίγος μὲν ἔην λινοβώρηξ.

"Ajax the Less a linen Thorax had."

Alexander, we are told by Plutarch, had θώρακα λινοῦν διπλοῦν, a two-fold linen thorax; and Iphicrates ordered his troops to lay aside their thoraces of steel for such as were made of hemp.[1] Brass, iron, and other metals were, however, the ordinary materials of which the thoraces were manufactured. In the British Museum is a fragment of a brass one, being the part which lay on the chest: it is covered with embossed ornaments in the shape of rings, &c. Strutt says, "Homer, speaking of the Greeks, frequently calls them the *brazen tunic-wearers*, Αχαιων χαλκοχιτωνων;[2] it is, however, very extraordinary, that, where he speaks at large concerning the warlike habits of his heroes, he has not specified this tunic, nor given us the least hint respecting its form. In the long description of Agamemnon arming himself for the battle,[3] we do not find it mentioned, unless the words by which this description is introduced may be thought applicable to it, "He also clothed himself in splendid brass," first about his legs he placed the handsome greaves, neatly joined with clasps of silver; then the thorax, on which Homer bestows ten lines. There is no mention of the tunic of brass in the request made by Thetis to Vulcan, for a new suit of armour to equip her son, neither is it noticed in the description of the arms as they were made by that deity; nor in a subsequent passage, where Achilles is described putting them on. But let us suppose that the thorax and the chalcochiton were only two denominations for the same armour, and we shall meet with no further difficulty. Strutt gives a figure[4] with the thorax large enough to cover not only the breast but all the front, at least, of the body, down to the navel, and probably it extended over the back in the same manner: the shoulder parts are fastened in the front with thongs, or cords, to the bottom of the thorax, and might, I presume, when those ligatures were unloosed, be thrown back at pleasure, so that the arms might easily be withdrawn, and the armour put off over the head of the wearer, and there are several passages in the antient poets that justify this opinion. In this example we observe appended to this breastplate several straps of leather,[5] perhaps plated with metal, (lambrequins,) reaching nearly to the bottom of the inner garment. In fact, I conceive the thorax to have been a large breastplate of brass affixed to a short sleeveless tunic, made of leather or some other appropriate material, to which the shoulder-guards were connected at the back. Hesiod, describing the arms of Hercules, says, he placed on his shoulders αρης αλκτηρα σιδηρον, the harm-repelling iron;[6] the thorax might also be laced on behind. That of Agamemnon, according to Homer, was splendidly ornamented, having upon it ten rows of black cyanus, μελανος κυανοιο,[7] twelve of gold, twenty of tin, enclosed by three azure dragons, κυανεοι δρακοντες τρεις, rising from either side of the pectoral, in the form of a rainbow. The thorax of Menelaus is said to have been διπλοος, or two-fold, having a girdle plated with brass beneath it, ηδ' ὑπενερθεν ζωμα τε καί μιτρη.[8] Agamemnon also had a variegated belt, strengthened with plates of silver under his pectoral, which repelled the point of a weapon that had passed through the latter, ζωνην θωρηκος ενέρθε."[9] Plutarch speaks of one that may be considered as of the mixed kind: he tells us,[10] that Zoilus, an armourer, having made a present of a thorax to Demetrius Poliorcetes, had it placed for an experiment of its hardness, about twenty-six paces from a catapulta, from which was discharged an arrow; this, so far from piercing the iron,

[1] Cornelius Nepos in Vità Iphic. The Latin word, however, being lorica, the μίτρη, and not the thorax, may be implied. The passage is as follows, "Idem genus loricarum mutavit et pro ferreis atque æneis linteas dedit. Quo facto expeditiores milites reddidit, nam pondere detracto, quod æquè corpus tegeret et bene esset curavit."

[2] Iliad, Lib. III, v. 127, 131, et alibi.

[3] At the beginning of the 11th book of the Iliad.

[4] In Strutt's Introduction to the Dress and Habits of the English. Pl. VII.

[5] These straps of leather to the termination of the breast-plate, and those depending from over the shoulders, the Chevalier Brönsted conceives to be the πτέρυγες.

[6] V. 128.

[7] Iliad, Lib. XI, v. 24.

[8] Iliad, Lib. IV, v. 156, 187; compare also 215 and 216.

[9] Ibid. XI, 235; and in 237 it is called ζωστηρ παναιολος.

[10] In Demetrio.

scarcely made the slightest impression on it. We are further told that it consisted of two parts, one of which being of iron and inflexible, was called *θώραξ στάδιος*, or *στάτος*, the stiff-standing thorax before noticed, the other was of a beast's hide, and, according to the poet,

. . . . ῷ δε θώρακος σκύτει.

"............ the skin of the thorax."

The iron part was probably a collar to the thorax, for such appears represented on a warrior crouching behind his shield, in Hope's Costume of the Antients.[1] The thoraces were, however, sometimes of linen covered with little scales of metal, and of this kind that worn by Minerva, always appears to be, or they were covered with flat rings, a custom that prevailed even with the Græco-Roman soldiers of Justinian, as appears by a Mosaic at Ravenna. In these cases they were called *θώρακες ἀλυσιδωτοί*, thoraces of chain-work, *λεπιδωτοί*, scaled, *φολιδωτοί*, plumated, &c., and occur in Hope's Costume.[2] *'Αλυσιδωτοί*, therefore, which literally means indissoluble, and thence expresses chain-work, probably consisted of several rows of rings fastened into each other, and stitched upon linen. Two such of brass, of the size of large curtain rings, may be seen in the British Museum. The lorica hamata too, of the Romans, appears to have been of rings cut through in one part, and hooked into linen cuirasses; the Greek one, Pl. IV, Fig. 19. seems to have been of this kind, and the rings are placed like rustred armour of the 12th century. Pausanias says, he saw the brazen thorax of Cleostratus, and it was thick set with hooks turned upwards. The only way to understand this passage, as it appears to me, is by imagining the rings in Fig. 19 to be reversed.

The warrior completed the equipments for his body by putting on the girdle to which was attached the drapery, at once the appendage of decency and elegance. Thus, Homer says,

Λῦσε δέ οἱ ζωστῆρα παναίολαν, ἠδ' ὑπένερθε
Ζῶμά τε καὶ μίτρην, ἣν χαλκῆες κάμον ἄνδρες.

"He then unbraced his rich embroidered belt, and underneath it placed
His zoma, and his mitree, which the workers of brass had made."

From the specimens Mr. Hope has given from the Greek vases, the embroidery, ornaments, or studs, on these girdles, were varied with considerable taste. As the act of putting on the girdle made the armour secure, *ζώννυσθαι*, to gird, became a general word to imply putting on armour. Hence, when Agamemnon commands the Greeks to arm, Homer says[3],

'Ατρείδης δὲ βοήσεν, ἰδὲ ζώννυσθαι ἄνωγεν.

"Atrides then shouted and commanded them to be girt."

The same poet, when he makes that hero resemble the god of war, in his *ζωνη*, or military belt, is supposed, according to Pausanias, to mean his whole armour. In the following passage, we have all these several parts enumerated:

Αὐτὴ δ' αὐτ' ἴθυνεν ὅθι ζωστῆρος ὀχῆες
Χρύσειοι σύνεχον, και διπλόος ἤντετο θώρηξ,
Εν δ' ἔπεσε ζωστῆρι ἀρηρότι πικρός ὀϊστός
Διὰ μὲν ἂρ ζωστῆρος ἐλήλατο δαιδαλέοιο,
Καὶ διὰ θώρηκος πολυδαιδάλου ἠρήρειστο,
Μίτρης θ', ἣν ἐφόρει ἔρυμα χροὸς, ἕρκος ἀκόντων
Η οἱ πλεῖστον ἔρυτο.

"But she directed it to that part where the golden straps of the belt were held together,
And where the two-fold thorax met it.
On his belt, well fitted, fell the piercing arrow,
And through the well-wrought belt it passed,

[1] Pl. LXVI. [2] Pl. XLVII, L, &c. [3] Iliad, λ. [4] Iliad, δ.

And in the thorax, curiously wrought, infixed it stands;
And in the mitree, which he wore as the safeguard to his body,
And which protected him most."

The belt in this case was not worn just above the loins, but just below the chest, as in Hamilton's Etruscan Antiquities.[1] But besides this body-armour the Greeks[2] had protections for their legs, which rose in front to the top of their knees, nearly met behind at the calves, and terminated just above the ankles: these were called *κνημῖδες*, greaves, and were of metal, as brass, tin, &c. Thus Hesiod,[3]

. . . . κνημῖδας ὀρϑίχαλκοιο φαεινοῦ
Ἡφαίστοῦ κλυτὰ δῶρα, περὶ κνήμησιν ἔϑηκεν.

" . . . . The greaves of shining brass,
The famous gift of Vulcan, he round his knees placed."

And Homer,[4]

Τεῦξε δέ οἱ κνημῖδας ἑανοῦ κασσιτέροιο.

" He made his greaves of beaten tin."

But Laërtes, the father of Ulysses, is described[5] as wearing them of bull's hide. When put on they were closed behind, being elastic, with pieces of metal terminating in buttons.[6] To this also Homer refers,

Κνημῖδας μὲν πρῶτα περὶ κνήμησιν ἔϑηκε
Καλὰς, ἀργυρέοισιν ἐπισφυρίοις ἀραρυίας.

" But first round his knees the greaves he put,
Which were beautiful,[7] fitted with silver buttons."

So general was the use of this piece of armour, that Homer perpetually calls the Greeks

. . . ἐϋκνήμῖδες Ἀχαιοί.

". . . . Well-greaved Greeks."

We read of *χείριδες*, or guards for the hands, but though these were partially used, I have not met with any representation of them.

The original Greek shield was the *ασπις*, a word which literally implies covering, and their form was *εὔκυκλοι πάντοτε ἴσαι*, perfect circles, equal in every direction; they were convex, which part was termed *ἀντύξ*, and edged with a broad flat rim, called *περιφέρεια*, or *κύκλος*, the circumference or circle, and the edge of this was denominated *ἴτυς*, the extremity. The centre had on it a projecting convex part, called *ὀμφάλος*, and *μεσομφάλιον*, from its resemblance to the navel: upon this was sometimes placed another projection, termed *ἐπομφάλιον*, which is said to have been of great service in repelling missile weapons, by occasioning them to glance off, and also for bearing down their enemies.[8] Across, within side the shield, was placed a band of metal under which passed the arm, forming with it the letter *χ*,[9] said to have been invented by the Carians, and called *ὄχανον*, or

[1] Vol. IV, Pl. XXX. The Chevalier Brönsted conceives that curved piece of bronze about a foot in length, four inches and a half across the centre, made at one end with a hook and at the other with appliances for a strap, and ornamented with little bosses to be the *μίτρη*. He has given a plate of one he possessed, now in the Bibliotheque du Roi at Paris, in his magnificent work on the Bronzes of Siris.

[2] All the figures in armour which appear on the Elgin marbles are in cuirasses exactly resembling those worn by the Romans, but without lambrequins; they are, therefore, probably of leather. A figure of Mars, Pl. XLVIII, of Hope's Costume, in the old, or severe style, is thus accoutred.

[3] Scuto.

[4] Iliad, *τ'*. v. 612.

[5] Hom. Odys. Lib. XXV, v. 228.

[6] See Hope's Costume of the Antients, Pl. LXX.

[7] Several of the specimens in Hope's Costume fully justify the epithet, and it is to be recollected, that Homer only applies it to those of the commanders.

[8] These several parts are fully shewn in the specimens given by Mr. Hope.

[9] See Hope's Costume, Pl. LXVII; and Eustathius' Iliad, *β*. p. 184, edit. Basil.

ὄχανη, while the hand grasped one of the *κανόνες*, which were festooned all round the edge of the concave circumference, or at other times these were omitted for cords attached to little rings, and called *πόρπακες*, two of which crossed the arm, while a handle was held in the hand.[1] Such handles, when the wars were ended, and the shields, as was the custom, hung up in the temples of the Gods, were removed to render them unfit for use, in case of a sudden insurrection : hence Aristophanes introduces a person affrighted, who exclaims when he sees the shields hanging up with the handles,

Οἴ μοι τάλας, ἔχουσι γὰρ πόρπακας.

"Oh! woe is me, for the shields have handles on."

Sometimes the shield was furnished with a thong of leather, by which it was hung on the shoulder ; but though I do not recollect its application any where illustrated, I think it appears on that of Theseus, where he is represented in a contest with the Amazons, on a fictile vase.[2] Homer, however, thus mentions it,[3]

. . . . . αὐτὰρ ἀπ' ὤμων
Ασπὶς σὺν τελαμῶνι χαμαὶ πέσε τερμιοεσσα.

". . . . But from his shoulders
The shield, reaching to the feet with its thong, fell on the ground."

Æschylus speaks of little bells hung from the shields to strike terror into an enemy,

. . . . ἀπ' ἀσπίδος δε τῷ
Χαλκήλατοι πλάζουσι κώδωνες φοβῳ.

". . . . . From the shields
The brazen bells put them to flight through fear."

But of this kind I have seen no representation.

These shields were most tastefully ornamented with tripods, serpents, scorpions, and other mythological subjects, surrounded by elegant borders, as may be seen in Hope's Costume of the Antients. This custom, according to Herodotus, was first introduced by the Carians, and from them communicated to the other Grecian states, the Romans, and the Barbarians. According to Polynæus, the Lacedemonians on a particular occasion had their names engraven on their shields.[4]

Pausanias tells us, that "he saw in the treasury of Olympia a shield covered with laminæ of brass, and adorned inside with various pictures, together with a helmet and greaves ; the inscription on these arms implied, that they were spoils dedicated by the Myones. On the tomb of Epaminondas is his shield, on which is embossed a dragon, which implied that he was descended from those called Sparti, who are said to have originated from the teeth of a dragon."

All these remarks have been confined to the large round buckler, called aspis, which was made of several folds of leather, whence it was called *ἀσπὶς βόεια*. It was covered with plates of metal, which were laid one over the other, hence Achilles' buckler is thus described.[5]

. . . . . πέντε πτύχας ἤλασε Κυλλοποδίων,
Τὰς δύο χαλκείας, δύο δ' ἔνδοθι κασσιτέροιο,
Τὴν δε μίαν χρυσῆν.

". . . . . . With five plates Vulcan forged it,
With two of brass, two within those of tin,
And one of gold."[6]

1 See Hope's Costume, Pl. CIV.

2 Ibid. Pl. XXII ; and Hamilton's Etruscan Antiquities, Vol. II, Pl. CXXVI. The warrior appears in a quilted tunic.

3 Iliad. ρ'. It served the purpose of the guige of the middle ages.

4 Lib. I, c. 17.

5 Iliad, ύ. 270.

6 These may have extended beyond each other so as to display the whole.

And that of Ajax as,[1]

> . . . σάκος αἰόλον, ἑπταβόειον
> Ταύρων ζατρεφέων, ἐπὶ δ' ὄγδοον ἤλασε χαλκόν.
>
> " . . . . Made of the hides of seven
> Well-fatted bulls, and covered with a plate of brass the eighth."

There appears in several representations, on fictile vases, a piece of drapery suspended from the shield, the intention of which seems to have been, to break the force of any cut made at the legs, and it was probably used before the invention of greaves; it does not occur however in the Elgin marbles, where none of the figures wear greaves, while it is depicted on vases as held by warriors which often have those protections.[2] It occurs generally with the evil eye painted on it, under the superstitious idea, that it would work mischief to those that beheld it.

The aspis appears to have been about three feet in diameter, for in the specimens given by Mr. Hope,[3] they reach from the neck to the calf of the leg; hence, Tyrtæus says,

> Μηρούς τὲ, κνήμας τὲ κάτω καὶ στέρνα, καί ὤμης,
> Ἀσπιδος ἐυρείης γαςτρὶ καλυψάμενος.
>
> " Having covered the thighs, legs, breast, and shoulders
> With the hollow of the broad shield."

On this account Homer calls them ἀμφιβροτας, and ποδηνηκείς, the warriors often, by kneeling down and bending their heads, concealing themselves behind them.[4] Pollux[5] mentions an aspis κοίλη ἑτερομηκης, with an edge or keel longer in one place then another, but unless this refers to the flat part being prolonged at the top and bottom, to make the shield an oval,[6] while the central part was circular, I am unable to comprehend it.

The aspis was generally carried by the heavy armed infantry, and those who fought in chariots. The cavalry had a much lighter and smaller round shield,[7] composed of a hide with the hair on, and called λαισήϊον, from λάσιος, hairy. Homer notices their lightness,

> . . . . βοέιας
> Ἀσπίδας εὐκύκλους, λαισήϊα τε πτερόεντα.
>
> " . . . . The bull's-hide
> Well-rounded aspida, and the light laiseia."

Polyænus[8] mentions an iron shield in the time of the Seleucidæ in Persia, as having been thrown up as a signal for the Macedonian and Thracian horse to massacre the Persians. A small convex bronze shield is among the Hamilton Antiquities in the British Museum.

The light infantry were armed according to Xenophon, with the πελτὴ, a shield resembling an ivy-leaf, and borrowed from the Amazons. The companion of Ajax, the son of Oileus, is depicted with one of these on a fictile vase in Sir William Hamilton's collection, now in the British Museum.[9] The γεῤῥον or γεῤῥα, was a fiddle-shaped shield, imitated from those of the Persians, as we are told by Strabo,[10] a fact that sufficiently appears by comparing those sculptured at Persepolis with those represented in Hope's Costume.[11] They were adopted by the Thebans. The Greeks also used an oblong shield, called θυρεός, from its resemblance to a gate, being curved on its upper line,

[1] Iliad, ή. 222.

[2] It is singular that the Mexicans are the only people who had a similar custom.

[3] See Costume of the Antients, Pl. LXVI, LXVIII. and LXX.

[4] Ibid. Pl. LXVI; and Polyænus mentions, that under cover of their shields they sometimes dug trenches to ensnare the cavalry: Lib. II, c. iii.

[5] Lib. I, C. X.

[6] There is an oval shield, however, in Hamilton's Etruscan Antiquities, Vol. III, Pl. CVIII, where two prize-fighters are represented on a stage.

[7] See one of these placed on three cavalry lances on a frieze engraved at the top of p. 47, Vol. III, of Stuart's Antiquities of Athens. From this the diameter appears to have been rather less than two feet.

[8] Lib. VII, c. xxxix.

[9] See Vol. III, Pl. LVII, of the Etruscan Antiquities.

[10] Lib. XV.

[11] Pl. LXXVI, CIV, and CXXVI.

and pierced to look through, or to carry on the spear. I have not seen any one of these in Grecian representations, but it occurs in the Græco-Egyptian paintings on the walls of the tombs of the kings at Thebes.[1]

To lose the shield was accounted the greatest disgrace, hence Epaminondas, in the agonies of death, inquired for the safety of his shields; and the Spartan mothers desired their sons either to bring back their bucklers, or be brought upon them.

For close fight the arms of the Greeks were clubs, *φάλαγγες*, the mace, *κορύνη*, the spear, *ἔγχος*, the lance, *δόρυ*, the pole-axe, *ἀξίνη*, the battle-axe, *πέλεκυς*, the sword, *ξίφος*, and the dagger, *μάχαιρα*. As the clubs were used in close fight, compact bodies of troops, called phalanxes, are thence supposed to have derived that denomination. Polyænus tells us, that Pisistratus, the tyrant of Athens, had a guard of 300 men armed with clubs.[2] This primitive weapon soon, however, gave way to the mace, which had its name from the little horns or spikes by which its head was surrounded. Periphetes, slain by Theseus, was named *κορυνήτης*, from using this weapon,[3] and the same appellation is given by Homer to Areithous, for the same reason.[4]

Δίυ 'Αρηϊθόυ τὸν ἐπίκλησιν, κορυνήτην
Ανδρες κίκλεσκον καλλίζωνὶ τε γυναῖκες,
Οὔνεκ' ἄρ' οὐ τοξοισι μαχέσκετο, δυρί τε μακρῷ,
'Αλλὰ σιδηρέιῃ κορύνῃ ῥήγνυσκε φάλαγγας.

"The title of the God-like Areithous, mace-bearer,
Men and beautiful-zoned women celebrate,
Because he never used bows nor long lance,
But with his iron mace whole squadrons routed."

One of these maces in a horseman's hand occurs on an old Greek coin, engraved in Stuart's Antiquities of Athens;[5] and several brazen mace-heads, which prove that the handle was generally of wood, may be seen in the British Museum.[6]

The spear was generally of ash, with a leaf-shaped head of metal, and furnished with a pointed ferrule at the but, called *σαυρωτήρ*, with which it was stuck in the ground, a method adopted according to Homer, when the troops rested on their arms, or when sleeping on their shields.[7] Pausanias saw in the Temple of Minerva a spear, attributed to Achilles, the blade and ferrule of which were of brass.[8] It was the custom to put the spears against a column when not used, whence originated fluted pillars, hence Homer says,

Ἔγχος ὁ μὲν ἔστησε φέρων πρὸς κίονα μακρὸν
Δυροδόκης ἔντοσθεν ἐΰξόον.

"Bringing his well-finished spear he placed it against a high column,
And filling the fluting made to hold pikes."

The Macedonians had a particularly long spear, called *σάρισσα*, which was fourteen or sixteen cubits in length. Polyænus says, the people of Edessa had the same, but that, at the siege of that city, Cleonymus, who led them, ordered his front line to use no arms, but with both hands to seize the spears of their enemy, and hold them fast while the next rank advanced within and closed upon them: their spears having been thus seized the men retreated, but the next rank pressing on them gained the victory. By

[1] See Denon's Egypt, Pl. LV; and Pl. I, of this work.
[2] Strat. Lib. I, c. xxi.
[3] Plutarch in Theseo: and Diod. Sic. Lib. IV.
[4] Iliad, *η*. v. 136.
[5] Vol. III, p. 53.
[6] With these are many that were not thus used, but placed on the striker of a flail, several in succession, made to fit its increasing diameter towards its end, to prevent their flying off, and some of this kind are to be seen in the armoury at Goodrich Court, Herefordshire. Such a military weapon was used by the Portuguese till the conclusion of the 16th century.
[7] Iliad, v. 151. Aristotle de Arte Poetica. This ferrule is perceptible in the examples given in Hope's Costume.
[8] Plutarch tells us that a bronze spear head, and sword, were found in the grave of Theseus. His words are, *Εὑρέθη δὲ θήκητε μεγάλου σώματος αἰχμή τε παρακειμένη χαλκή και ξίφος.* In vita Thes.

this manœuvre the long and formidable spear was rendered useless, and was considered an encumbrance rather than a weapon of offence.[1]

The doru, or lance, was probably that used by the cavalry, and furnished with a loop of leather which served the warrior for a support when he chose to let it hang from his arm, and to twist round his hand for the firmer grasp when charging: this strap was called μεσάγκυλη, being put on about the middle. Three of these lances, with the laiseion, or small shield, may be seen represented in Stuart's Antiquities of Athens.[2]

The axine was a staff, on the end of which was a spike, with an axe-blade on one side, and another spike on the other.[3] With this weapon Agamemnon is said to have encountered Pisander.[4]

> . . . . ὁ δ' ὑπ' ἀσπίδος εἵλετο καλὴν
> Ἀξίνην εὔχαλκον, ἐλαΐνῳ ἀμφὶ πελέκκῳ
> Μακρῷ, εὐξέστῳ.

> " . . . . But he from under his shield drew forth a beautiful
> Axine, of well-tempered brass, and in its blade a shaft of olive,
> Long and beautifully worked."

The pelekus had a short handle, and at its top an axe-blade, with a pike opposite.[5] Homer mentions it as indiscriminately used with the axine.[6]

> Ἀλλ' οἵ γ' ἐγγύθεν ἱστάμενοι, ἕνα θυμὸν ἔχοντες
> Ὀξέσι δὴ πελεκέσσι, καὶ ἀξίνῃσι, μάχοντο,

> " Both parties close together stood, and with one mind fought
> With keen-edged axes, and with axines."

The xiphos, or sword, was worn at the left hip, suspended by a leathern strap that passed over the right shoulder, and thus it appears on several fictile vases.[7] Hence, Hesiod says,[8]

> Ὤμοισιν δέ μιν ἀμφὶ μελάνδετον ἄορ ἔκειτο
> Χάλκεον ἐκ τελαμῶνος.

> " Round about his shoulders hung
> A brazen dark-bound sword from the belt."[9]

And Homer,[10]

> Ἀμφὶ δ' ἄρ ὤμοισιν βάλετο ξίφος ἀργυρόηλον.

> " About his shoulder hung the silver-studded sword."

The xiphos was straight, intended for cutting and thrusting, with a leaf-shaped blade, and not above twenty inches in length, it therefore reached only to the thigh, a circumstance noticed by the accurate Homer.[11]

> . . . . φάσγανον ὀξὺ ἐρυσσάμενος παρὰ μηροῦ.

> " . . . . . Having drawn the sharp sword from his thigh."

It had no guard, but a cross bar, which, with the κολεὸς, or scabbard, was beautifully ornamented.[12]

The makaira, or dagger, was more frequently used as a knife, but worn in the scabbard of the sword. Homer thus describes it.[13]

> Ἀτρείδης δὲ ἐρυσσαμενος χείρεσσι μάχαιραν,
> Ἥ οἱ πὰρ ξίφεος μέγα κουλεὸν αἰὲν ἄορτο.

> " Atrides having drawn the dagger with his hands,
> Which in the wide scabbard of his sword was ever hung."

1 Strat. Lib. II, c. xxix.
2 Vol. III, p. 47.
3 See it in Hope's Costume, Pl. LII, Fig. 3.
4 Iliad, ύ. 611.
5 See Hope's Costume, Pl. XX.
6 Iliad, ύ. 710.
7 See Hope's Costume, Pl. LXX, LXXXI, and CII.
8 Scuto Herculis.
9 Pausanias saw in the temple of Æsculapius the sword of Memnon among the Nicomedenses, and it was wholly of brass.
10 Iliad, β'.
11 Odyss. γ'.
12 Pausanias says that in the treasury of Olympia was preserved the sword of Pelops, the hilt of which was of ivory and gold.
13 Iliad, γ.

The sword used by the Argives was called κοπὶς, and, from its name, seems to have been principally employed for striking;[1] those of the Lacedemonians, according to Pollux, ξυίναι, or, as Xenophon has it, ξυήλαι; and those of the Athenians κνήστιες; all of which were of the short cutting kind.[2] At a later period of the Grecian history, the akinakes, or long curved dagger, with its edge on the inner curve, was borrowed from the Persians.[3]

Besides what have been enumerated, the Greeks had several missile weapons, these were slings, javelins, and bows.

The σφενδονη, or sling, was especially the weapon of the Acarnanians,[4] the Ætolians,[5] and the Achæans,[6] who inhabited Ægium, Dyma, and Patræ, but the last of these so far excelled, that when anything was directly levelled at a mark, it was usual to call it Αχαῖκον βέλος.[7] It was sometimes made of wool,[8] and sometimes of leather, and is described by Dionysius[9] as having its cup not exactly hemispheroidical, but hemispheroidical, decreasing to two thongs at its ends. Out of it were cast stones or plummets of lead, called μολυβδίδες, or μολυβδίναι σφαῖραι, some of which are engraved by Stuart, on the upper part of page 27, in the third volume of his Antiquities of Athens: they are spheroidical, having an ornament on one side, and the word δέξας on the other. We are told that some of these weighed no less than an Attic pound, i. e. an hundred drachms.[10] According to their size the slings were managed by one, two, or three cords. At a later period the Greeks had a method of casting from their slings, πυροβόλοι λίθοι, or fire-balls, and from their machines, σκυτάλια, made of combustibles, fitted to an iron head, which, being armed with a pike, stuck fast into its object, while it set the same on fire.[11]

The different sorts of javelins were the γρόσφος, the αιγανεα, and the υσσὸς, and the form of their heads may be seen in the Vignette, page 27, Vol. III, of Stuart's Antiquities of Athens. Several of these were loose upon their shafts, in all probability having attached to them a cord, which was held by the side of the wood, so that when the weapon once entered the body, the head could not be extracted without the greatest difficulty. I am led to this conclusion from an Asiatic javelin, in my own collection, on a similar principle, and which, like them, has just below the blade, a hook turned backward, to prevent its being withdrawn; and because some of the Greek javelins, according to their writers, are said to have been furnished with a cord, called ἀγκυλη.

The τόξον, or bow, was the favourite weapon of the Cretans.[12] Lycophron[13] and Theocritus[14] speak of the Mæotian, or Scythian bow, which, we learn from Athenæus, was in the form of the letter C, like that now used by the Tartars. The Greek bow, on the other hand, was made of two long goat's-horns, fitted into a handle:[15] hence, Lycophron says,

. . . . ἐν χάρμαισι ῥαιβώσας κερας.

". . . . In battles having bent his horn."

The original bow strings were thongs of leather, whence Homer tells us,

Ἕλκε δ' ὁμοῦ γλυφίδας τε λαβὼν καὶ τόξα βόεια.

"He drew, taking hold at the same time of the nocks and bow of ox-horn."

1 There is a figure in Hamilton's Etruscan Antiquities with a cutting sword like a hanger: this figure has the belt at the bottom of the thorax. Vol. IV, Pl. xxx.

2 Plutarch tells us, that the shortness of the sword was ridiculed to Agesilaus by a person who said a juggler would make nothing of swallowing it; from which it appears, that this trick, practised by the Indian jugglers, is of great antiquity.

3 Moschopolus in voc. Att. Pollux, &c. It may be seen in the hands of some Græco-Roman gladiators, on a lamp, in Montf. Antiq. expl. Vol. V, Pl. cxcvii.

4 Pollux, Lib. i, cap. x.

5 Strabo.

6 Livy, Lib. xxxviii.

7 Suidas.

8 Homer's Iliad, ν'. 599.

9 περιήγησις, v. 5.

10 Small ones may be seen in the British Museum, and at Goodrich Court.

11 Suidas.

12 Diodorus Sic. and Isidorus.

13 Cassandra, v. 914.

14 Idyll. xiii. v. 956. One may be seen on a vase in Hamilton's Etruscan Antiquities, Vol. IV, Pl. cxvi.

15 Homeri, Iliad, δ. v. 105.

But afterwards horse-hair was substituted, which occasioned their being called ἵππεια;[1] and they were formed of three plaits, whence they were also named τρίκωσις. The ends of the bow were termed κορῶναι, and were generally of gold, and, indeed, the bows were ornamented with gold and silver also on other parts. The arrow heads were sometimes pyramidal, whence the epithet τετράγονα;[2] and the shafts were furnished with feathers. They were carried in a quiver, which, with the bow, was slung behind the shoulders: thus Apollo in Homer,[3] is represented as

Τόξ᾽ ὤμοισιν ἔχων, ἀμφηρεφέα τε φαρέτρην.

"Carrying his bow and quiver on his shoulders."

Some of these were square, some round, many had a cover to protect the arrows from dust and rain, and many appear on fictile vases to have been lined with skins. As the Greek bows were small, they were drawn not to the ear but to the right breast, which Homer thus describes,

Νευρὴν μὲν μάζῳ πέλασεν, τόξῳ δε σίδηρον

"Up to his breast he drew the string, and to the bow the iron head of the arrow."

I have not found any passage in the antient writers, nor discovered any representation, to authorize the conclusion that the Greek archers, like those of Mexico and many modern American tribes, made use of the shield, though sculptures on the Trajan column shew that it was not an unusual custom with slingers. There is, however, in the British Museum, a sculpture in marble, of a collection of arms, which appear to have been merely for one man, and are of the same size as the originals: this consists of a pair of greaves, made exactly to fit the legs and projecting bones of the knees, above them a helmet, and on the right side a bow, and an oval shield, rather more than two feet in its greatest diameter, and having a boss in the centre.[4]

Plate IV consists of Greek arms and armour. Fig. 1, is the Theban shield, copied from the Persian Gerra. Fig. 2, a Theban bow-case and quiver united. Fig. 3, a Greek bow in its case. Fig. 4, the double-headed lance of the cavalry, taken from an equestrian figure on a lamp in Montfaucon's Antiq. expl.[5] Fig. 8, the laiseion, or equestrian shield, from the frieze of an Athenian temple. Across Fig. 4, is the long spear of the infantry. Fig. 5, the inside and outside of a greave for the right leg. Fig. 6, the aspis. Fig. 7, the inside of ditto, exhibiting the ockanon and the canones. Fig. 9, 10, 11, and 12, various Greek helmets. Fig. 10, one with three crests, or eminences, seen in front. Fig. 14, the xiphos, or straight sword. Fig. 21, the kopis, having its edge on the inner curve of the blade. Fig. 16, the xiphos without the scabbard. Fig. 20, the sheath of the kopis. Fig. 15, a Greek quiver. Fig. 17, a Greek bow. Fig. 18, a cuirass, worn by the warrior who uses the kopis, and which exhibits the girdle as passing over the ends of the shoulder-pieces. Fig. 19, a cuirass of quilted linen, covered with a mitree of rustres, above which is the complete thorax of two pieces, and below the zone, or girdle.

ETRUSCAN ARMOUR.

As the Etruscans were colonies from Greece we can not expect to find much difference in regard to their armour, but we derive the confirmation of such a curious fact from the bronzes and fictile vases discovered in that part of Italy which they inhabited, and we may perceive among them not only the remains of the antient Grecian style of armour, but subsequent changes unlike those of the parent country, and to which we may trace the origin of the Roman warlike habits.[6] The body-armour of the

1 Hesychius.

2 Some of these of different sizes are preserved in the armoury, at Goodrich Court.

3 Iliad, ά.

4 This curious antique relic was found in the plains of Marathon, and forms the centre of the Vignette in the title page of this work.

5 Tom. V, Pl. CXCVIII.

6 Strutt gives a representation of an Etruscan warrior in bronze, and notices a peculiar protection of grating, or network for his face, attached to his helmet, adding, that this is not the only specimen he had met with.

Plate IV.

GRECIAN ARMOUR.

ETRUSCAN ARMOUR.

Etruscans consisted of a helmet resembling those of the Greeks, a cuirass, plain, scaled, ringed, laminated, or quilted, and a thorax. They sometimes wore greaves,[1] which subsequently gave way to buskins, or sometimes had their legs quite unprotected.

Their shields were circular, much smaller than the aspis of the Greeks, and held by one handle in the centre, or else octagonal, but of that form that might be described in an acute angle subtended by a curve.[2] Their swords much resemble those of the Greeks, being short, with leaf-shaped blades, but the hilt had sometimes a guard, which encircled the hand, of a single bar. Dependent from their cuirasses were straps, sometimes merely of leather, in other instances with pieces of metal on them, and these appendages, termed by the French lambrequins, were, together with their plain and laminated cuirasses, adopted by the Romans. Some of their spear-men had a cap, probably of linen, which protected the throat, leaving the face only visible, like the capuchon of the Normans; and these, for armour, wore a quilted tunic with short sleeves.[3] Their archers had a cap and tunic of leather, and had twisted woollen cords round their legs, similar to those worn by the early Saxons.

Strutt thus describes his bronze Etruscan warrior, "He is clothed with a short tunic, having no skirts on the sides below the girdle. It is remarkable that the sleeve of the right arm is full of folds, and seems clearly not to belong to the tunic, while that of the left arm as evidently forms a part of it. The tunic, I presume, was made of leather, too thick and rigid to admit of sufficient liberty for the sword arm, and for that reason the sleeve, which probably belonged to the inner garment, was made of some more flexible material. These observations will also apply to a similar bronze in the possession of R. P. Knight, Esq." In reading this, one cannot help being struck with the resemblance to the Thracian retiarii.

Plate v, Fig. 5 and 6, are the cap and bow of an Etruscan archer. Fig. 7, an Etruscan shield seen on the inside. Fig. 8 and 9, two Etruscan helmets, the last five-crested, with the horse-tail besides. Fig. 10, a cuirass, with the thorax. Fig. 11, another, covered with rings. These two shew the shape of the single thorax. Fig. 12, a scaled cuirass, on which the thorax assumes the shape of merely two shoulder pieces. Fig. 13, a banded cuirass, with a singular thorax. Fig. 14, a cuirass apparently quilted.

ARMOUR OF THE SAMNITES.

Count Caylus, in the third volume of his Antiquities, has given among the Etruscan warriors, an armed Samnite; his helmet is something like the Greek pericephalaia, but instead of the visor forming a part of it, it is put on the face like a mask, perforated merely for the eyes, and comes down to the collar-bones, it is also furnished with a ridge. Beneath the helmet the warrior wears a gorget, and a breast and back piece of leather terminating at the shoulders, reaching to the hips with an indented edge, and strapped round the abdomen with two broad bands. Round his arms he wears

[1] In the small Etruscan bronze, figured by Strutt, that author observes, "they are exceedingly rough, and to all appearance made of the hides of some animal, being fastened behind by a single ligature over the middle of the calf." But the excavations at Herculaneum have proved that they were of bronze, and the workmanship extremely elegant. In the armoury at Goodrich Court, are a *περικεφαλή* from Herculaneum, a *κράνος* for infantry, in shape much like a morian, of the time of Queen Elizabeth, and an elegant *κόρυς* ornamented with a horse's head in relief, with a pair of greaves all of bronze, and found on the estate of the Prince of Canino, which if not Etruscan must be Greek. The splendour of the Etruscan armour may be seen in the outlines of those exquisitely executed engravings in the Museo Borbonico, Pl. LVIII, and LX. of Vol. III, Pl. XXIX, and XLIV. of Vol. IV. (particularly the latter), Pl. XXIX of Vol. V. Pl. XIV of Vol. VII. Pl. XXXII, XXXVI, XXXVII, and XXXVIII of Vol. VIII. and XXXI, of Vol. X.

[2] In my own possession is a little bronze figure, between three and four inches high, with a shield, of the kite shape, extending from his shoulder down to his feet; another, very similar, but with the shield only half its height, is also in my collection. These came from Naples. Qu. Were they Etruscan? They greatly resemble a figure in Montf. Antiq. expl. Vol. IV. Pl. XV, the shield of which, though not of the kite form, might be mathematically inscribed in it, it is likewise impressed with the figure of a griffin. Signor Campanari discovered in an Etruscan tomb at Vulsinum, a large bronze shield like the Greek *ασπις*. In his excavations there, he found the hilt of a sword of bronze, and spear-heads and sword-blades of iron; the first is now I believe in the British Museum, the rest in the possession of Mr. H. S. Cuming.

[3] See Hope's Costume, Pl. XL.

bracelets, and his legs are defended by boots which reach nearly to his knees. His sword is of the Greek fashion, leaf-shaped, and his shield, in shape, a portion of a cylinder.

This shield was afterwards adopted by the Romans, when the Samnites became incorporated with that people; at a later period, therefore, the Samnite equipments were used only by the gladiators, such, perhaps, as may have been of that nation.[1] In one of the tessellated pavements discovered at Bignor, in Sussex, is represented a combat between one of these and a retiarius; the helmet appears devoid of its ridge, and may have been only of leather, for the face-guard is of the colour of steel, while that is red and brown.

But we have another most interesting representation in the monument which the Emperor Caracalla erected to Bato. Dion Cassius, quoting Xiphilin, tells us, that that tyrant, having filled Rome with blood and murder, turned his thoughts to the public games, where, besides other cruelties, he took pleasure in the number of gladiators he caused to perish. He obliged one, named Bato, to fight successively three others on the same day. Bato was killed, and Caracalla had a fine monument erected to his memory. This monument was discovered in the Villa Pamphilia, bearing the simple but comprehensive inscription "BATONI." His helmet is on a tree, having a small ridge, and the perforations in the visor circular; instead of a gorget, if Fabretti's engraving be correct, he wears two straps of leather as necklaces, fastened in front with fibulæ: his body-armour is of the antient kind as first described, his shield a semi-cylinder, but rounded at the lower end, approaching to a point, the handles subtending its edges: on his legs are ornamented boots, reaching to the ankle and covering the instep, and over that on the left leg, is placed a plate of iron fixed upon a wadded wrapper, his sword is straight. Livy mentions this shield of the Samnite gladiators thus,[2] "Its form was broad in the upper part, the better to guard the breast and shoulders, and from this part towards the lower end of equal width, at the bottom, however, its form was wedge-like for the convenience of movement." He adds, "the covering for the chest was of sponge, a greave was bound on the left leg, and the helmet was crested."

Plate v, Fig. 1, is a Samnite cuirass and gorget. Fig. 2, a Samnite helmet. Fig. 3, another from Montf. Antiq. expl.[3] Fig. 4, a Samnite shield seen inside.

SICILIAN ARMOUR.

THE people of Sicily being of Greek and Carthaginian origin, their armour partakes of the character of both. There is a shield, helmet, and cuirass, with a figure of Perseus, in Montf. Antiq. expl.[4] The shield is octagonal, with a boss in the centre, but the sides are by no means equal, indeed, it might be mathematically inscribed in the long kite shape. The helmet is a mere scullcap, with a bird's wing on each side; and the cuirass is like that of the antient Greeks, consisting of back and breast pieces, with lambrequins. In Vol. IV, of Montf. Pl. xv, Fig. 2, is a bronze figure, with a shield greatly similar, on which is engraved a griffin, and in my own possession, two much resembling this, with the shield absolutely kite-shaped. These came from Naples as has been already observed.

ROMAN ARMOUR.

THE Latin people, according to tradition, were composed of those wandering Trojans that had survived the destruction of their city, and the subjection of their country to the Greeks: from these, and the original Celtic inhabitants of Latium, Romulus collected and combined those predatory bands which became the parents of the Roman people. As the hardy Celtic race were without body armour, we should look in the earliest specimens of this new people for some traces of that which distinguished the Trojans. Our search is not without the expected result, for we find the head of Roma in the Phrygian helmet. But the Romans, once formed into a regular yet ambitious society, would naturally in time

[1] Livy says, (Lib. IX, c. xl,) that through hatred of the Samnites, the Campanians armed their gladiators after their manner. [2] Ibid. [3] Suppl. Vol. III, Pl. LXVII. [4] Vol. I, p. 146.

adopt the arts and characteristics of their more polished neighbours, hence we discover the Etruscan to be the principal style followed in Roman armies.[1]

The Romans were a nation of warriors, every citizen was obliged to enlist when the public service required, nor could any one enjoy an office who had not served ten campaigns.[2] Various alterations were subsequently made. In the purer times of the republic the cavalry were chosen from the equites or knights,[3] and the infantry from the next class, slaves and the lowest order being excluded, but Marius made a great alteration in the military system. After that period the cavalry was composed, not merely of Roman equites, but of horsemen raised from Italy and the other provinces; and the infantry consisted for the most part of the poorer citizens, or mercenary soldiers, which is justly reckoned one of the principal causes of the ruin of the republic. Under the Emperors indeed the Roman armies were chiefly formed of foreigners, the Celtiberians of Spain having been the first hired for pay.[4]

The Roman army was organized into legions, consisting of ten cohorts of infantry and ten troops of cavalry.

The foot were distinguished into heavy and light infantry: the former composed of the hastati, principes, and triarii, and the latter of the velites, funditores, and sagittarii. The cavalry into the equites, and the equites cataphracti. The hastati were so called, because at their origin they fought with hastæ, or long spears; and they probably formed the centre rank, they being able to reach beyond those of the front, but as they consisted of young men in the flower of life, they were afterwards appointed to the front rank:[5] when this alteration took place their long spears were laid aside as inconvenient.[6] In all the monuments, from the time of Titus to that of Theodosius, we meet with only one kind of spear, which appears little more than six feet long, it is carried both by the officers and soldiers. The Roman lance received an improvement while in Britain, and this being patronized by Lucullus, at that time governor of the island, who permitted them to be called "Lucullean lances," after his own name, afforded Domitian a pretext for putting him to death.[7]

The principes were men of middle age, and derived their name from having originally been posted first,[8] they afterwards, however, occupied the second rank.

The triarii were old soldiers of approved valour, who formed the third line. They were also sometimes called pilani, from the pilum, or javelin which they used: whence the hastati and principes who stood before them, were termed antepilani, and sometimes postsignani, from being placed in the rear of the principes, who carried the standard of the legion.

The arms both offensive and defensive of these three classes composing the heavy infantry, were much the same. The scutum, or shield, which was a hollow semi-cylinder, a convex hexagon, or that shape with its side angles rounded off, protected the hastati and principes. It was generally four feet long by two and a half broad,[9] made of wood joined together with little plates of iron, and the whole covered with a broad piece of linen, upon which was put a sheep's skin or bull's hide, having an iron boss jutting out in the centre. This contrivance was of great service in close fighting, whence, Martial says,

In turbam incideris, cunctos umbone repellat.

"If you should get in a crowd, let all be repelled by the boss."

The shields in more antient times were made of wicker, whence Virgil observes,[10]

. . . . Flectuntque salignas
Umbonem crates.

" . . . . And they bend the willows,
Putting a boss on the wicker."

1 Florus indeed, Lib. I, c. v, tells us, that Tarquin first introduced the Tuscan usages among the Romans.

2 Polyb. Lib. VI, 17.

3 Liv. Lib. V, 7.

4 Ibid. XXIV, 49. This was A.U.C. 537.

5 Livy. Lib. VIII. c. viii.

6 Varro de Ling. Lat. IV, 16.

7 Suet. in vit. Dom, s. 8.

8 Varro de Ling. Lat. IV. 16.

9 The longest about four feet nine inches.

10 Æneid, VII, 632.

The principes seem, however, sometimes to have used the clypeus, or round buckler. The triarii, generally carried it, though sometimes of a peculiar form, for in a drawing from the antique, in my possession, is one with a half pike in his right hand, and a shield on his left arm, apparently of leather, of a square form, but crimped into undulations. That he is a triarius is clear from his kneeling on his right knee, for, as Montfaucon observes, they awaited the signal of attack in this posture. They were all armed with a head-piece of brass or iron, called galea or cassis, with a flap behind which reached to the shoulders, but without any covering for the face :[1] hence, Cæsar, at the battle of Pharsalia, directed his men to strike at the face, faciem feri, Pompey's cavalry being principally composed of young men of rank, who prided themselves on their personal appearance.[2]

Originally the galea and cassis were two distinct headpieces, the former, like the lorica, being of leather, and the latter of metal but after this the terms were applied indifferently. The leathern cap seems to have fallen into disrepute in the time of Camillus, for according to Polyænus, in his Stratagems, "as the Gauls aimed the blows of the broad swords at the head, he made his men wear light helmets, by which their swords were blunted and broken; and the Roman shield being of wood, for the same reason he directed them to border it with a thin plate of brass. He also taught the use of the long spear, with which they engaged in close fight, and, receiving the blow of the sword with their shields made a thrust with the spear."

Upon the top of the helmet was sometimes merely a round knob, particularly on that of the common soldiers, and sometimes the crista, or crest, ornamented with plumes of feathers of various colours. Hence Virgil has,[3]

. . . . Cristâque tegit galea aurea rubrâ.

". . . . . And the golden helmet with a red crest covers him."

This helmet of the infantry was furnished with an umbril and two moveable cheek-pieces, which last were called Bucculæ. Hence Juvenal has,[4]

Fractâ de casside buccula pendens.

"The cheek-piece hanging broken from the helmet."

One of this kind in the British Museum has been engraved in the Vetusta Monumenta, and a similar one of bronze inscribed with the maker's name, and the word Roma is in the armoury at Goodrich Court. The body-armour was the lorica, which, like the French cuirass, was so called from having been originally made of leather,[5] and afterwards, like that, applied to metal: it followed the line of the abdomen at bottom, and seems to have been impressed while soft with marks corresponding to those of the human body ; at top the square aperture for the throat was guarded by the pectorale, or plate of brass, and the shoulders were in like manner protected by pieces made to slip over each other. Livy, speaking of Servius Tullius, says, "he armed the Romans with the galea, the clypeus, the ocreæ or greaves, and the lorica, all of brass."[6] This was the Etruscan attire, but several changes took place afterwards, and from the time of the republic greaves were not used, but the word ocreæ applied to the boots which succeeded them. On the Trajan column we find the lorica of the hastati and principes, consisting of several bands, each wrapping half round the body, and therefore fastening before and behind on a leathern or quilted tunic. In the British Museum some of these bands may be seen, and we thence learn that they were of brass, and about three inches wide. At a later period this was not the case, as Silius Italicus[7] has the expression,

. . . . . ferro circumdare pectus,

". . . . . . . To surround the breast with steel."

[1] Florus, IV, 2. A curious one, with a broad plate in front, is given by Montfaucon, in the Supplement to his Antiq. expl. Tom. IV, Pl. IX. In the same plate is a soldier with a cap like the Phrygian reversed.

[2] Florus, IV, 2. [3] Æn. IX, v. 49. [4] Sat. 10, v. 134.

[5] Varro says, "de corio crudo pectoralia faciebant." [6] Omnia ex ære. [7] Lib. VIII.

This laminated lorica was very heavy, and Tacitus informs us,[1] its weight was made a subject of complaint by some of the soldiers in the time of Galba, and even the Emperor himself, in his old age, found the weight of his cuirass too much for his feeble frame. It, however, was probably of the compact kind, for that writer further observes, that, when he was put to death, his murderers, finding his breast impenetrable from the armour which covered it, dissevered his legs and arms.[2] The Roman lorica was frequently enriched on the abdomen with embossed figures, on the breast with a Gorgon's head by way of amulet, on the shoulder-plates with scrolls of thunder-bolts, and on the leathern border which covered the top of the lambrequins with lions' heads: and these were formed of the precious metals, as the last quoted author tells us,[3] that some of the auxiliaries of Vitellius sold "their belts, accoutrements, and the silver ornaments of their armour." The compact cuirass was made to open at the sides, where the breast and back plates joined, by means of clasps and hinges. The boots of the Roman officers were laced before, and lined with the skin of some animal, of which the muzzle and claws were displayed as an ornamental finish. Each different legion had its peculiar device marked on its shields, and Tacitus alludes to this, when, describing the rebellion of Otho, and the effects of his inflammatory speech, he says, "having closed his harangue he ordered the magazine of arms to be thrown open. The soldiers seized their weapons, they paid no regard to military rules, no distinction was observed, the prætorians, the legions, and the auxiliaries crowded together, and shields and helmets were snatched up in a tumultuous manner."[4]

The loricæ of the triarii, appear to have been of leather only. From the column of Antonine we learn that, in the time of Marcus Aurelius, the oblong shield had almost altogether given way to the clypeus, while the triarii were clad in a cuirass of scales, or leaves of iron, called squammata. This had been first adopted from the Dacians, or Sarmatians, by the Emperor Domitian, who, according to Martial,[5] had a lorica made of boar's hoofs stitched together. Speaking of it, he says,

Quam vel ad Ætolæ securum cuspidis ictum,
Texuit innumeri lubricus unguis apri.

"Which secure even from the thrust of the Etolian spear,
He has covered with the polished hoofs of innumerable boars."

Virgil alludes to this scaled armour:[6]

. . . . . Rutilem thoraca indutus, ahenis
Horrebat squammis.

"Having put on the shining thorax, with brazen
Scales, he looked horrible."

And Plutarch tells us, that Lucullus wore *θώρακα σιδηροῦν φολιδωτον*, "a lorica made with pieces of iron shaped like the scales of a fish."

The clypeus again was laid aside in the time of Constantine, when the hexangular shields above-mentioned were used by the hastati.

The troops of the empire were clad in pantaloons that reached to the calves of their legs, but, in the time of the republic, they were bare-legged, like the modern Highlanders. Polybius, who wrote about 130 years before the Christian æra, thus speaks of these various troops, "the hastati were appointed to carry the arms, which they kept in their houses, their shields were four feet, or four and a half, long, by two and a half broad, bending round the bearer; they were made of two boards glued together, covered with a thick cloth glued in like manner, and over this a calf's skin, round it was a border of iron to defend it against all cutting strokes, and keep it in shape: in the midst an iron boss to sustain the blow of a stone, or the push of a lance or other weapon.[7] They had also a Spanish sword, which they wore on the right side, fit either for thrusting or cutting, with a strong well tempered

[1] Hist. Lib. I. [2] Hist. Lib. I. [3] Ibid. [4] Ibid. [5] Lib. VII. [6] Æn. XI, 487.

[7] This alludes more particularly to the iron plate, in the centre of which the boss was fixed.

blade edged on both sides. Moreover, they carry two great spears, some of which are thicker, others more slender; of the largest sort, the round ones are four fingers in diameter, and the others as much from side to side; the lesser sort resembles the ordinary Roman javelin, the shaft is three yards long, with an iron blade in the form of a hook, and pointed at the end,[1] of an equal length with the shaft; this iron, which reaches as far as the middle of the shaft, is firmly secured and riveted with nails, to prevent its being loosened or broken by any accident where it is joined. These soldiers wear a brass helmet, on the top of which is fastened a small coronet, or circle of iron, with three feathers, red and black in the middle, a foot and a half in length, which, towering so far above the head, make those who wear them appear big and terrible to their enemies: they have, moreover, protections for their legs and thighs. The ordinary soldiers wear on their breast a plate twelve inches each way, but those who are worth 10,000 drachmæ (or £150.) estate have, instead of this, a lorica. The principes and triarii have the same weapons, except that the latter, instead of javelins, use a kind of half pike."

Their sandals were called caligæ, being set with nails, or rather spikes, underneath, and from the wearing of which the Emperor Caligula had that name.[2] The centre and rear ranks had invariably swords, the long or short gladius, or ensis, and the triarii two pila, or javelins, each man: the swords were almost constantly worn on the right side, the principes wearing them at the hip, the triarii above it. In the time of the Emperor Theodosius the sword was so short that the blade was not above twice the length of the hilt, they were all of the stabbing kind, or rather cut and thrust; that carried by the generals was called parazonium, because worn near the girdle that surrounded the lorica just above the hips, it generally resembled the Lacedemonian swords, from whom, with its name, it was probably borrowed.

When the lorica was of one piece, whether of leather or metal, and reached to the abdomen, it had pendent from it several flaps, borrowed from the Etruscans, and these have been called by the French, lambrequins, they were of leather, fringed at the bottom, and sometimes highly ornamented. At the time of Trajan, the lorica was shortened, being cut straight round above the hips, and the bronze breast and back plates in the British Museum are of this style and period:[3] when this was the case there were two or three overlapping sets of lambrequins to supply the deficiency in length, and generals thus habited may be observed on the Trajan column.[4]

The light-armed troops were called by the general name of ferentarii, or rorarii,[5] and were, as before observed, of three kinds. The velites, so called from their agility, or the velocity with which they moved, were first instituted in the second Punic war;[6] they had no other protecting armour than a helmet and round shield, called parma,[7] about three feet in diameter, made of wood and covered with leather; they had no particular post assigned them, but fought in scattered parties as occasion required, usually before the lines. They each carried seven javelins, with points so slender that when thrown they bent, and could not easily be returned by the enemy,[8] by no means an unusual case; and a Spanish "cut and thrust" sword, cæsim et punctim. Polybius is particular in describing their javelin, he tells us "it had a wooden shaft, about two cubits long and a finger thick, to this was

[1] This description makes the Roman like a Persian weapon in the armoury, at Goodrich Court.

[2] Suet. in Vita Tacit. Ann. I. 41; Cic. Att. Lib. II. 3. See an engraving of them in Montf. Antiq. expl.

[3] It has been conjectured, that these were merely the shapes on which the moistened leather was stretched to give it the form of the human body, but as a person could have a free motion of his body in them, and as one of the buttons to which the shoulder-plates were fastened to hold the back and breast together still remains, it is put beyond any doubt that they formed the lorica actually worn. An engraving of these may be seen in Grose's Antient Armour. Besides, Pausanias, Lib. I, says "There were two pieces of brass, one which covered the chest and abdomen, the other the back." Compare them with two similar back and breast plates of bronze in the IVth. Vol. of the Museo Borbonico, Pl. XLIV.

[4] See Pl. CCXXV. of Hope's Costume of the Antients.

[5] Varro de Ling. Lat. Lib. VI. 3.

[6] Liv. Lib. XXVI. c. IV.

[7] Because "é medio in omnes partes sit par."

[8] Liv. XXIV. 34. In the month of June, 1824, in the centre of a square Roman Camp on Melon Hill, Gloucestershire, about three feet below the surface of the ground, 394 of the iron blades of such javelins were discovered, of which two are in the armoury at Goodrich Court. They are 30 inches in length, about three-quarters of an inch wide, and very thin.

affixed a blade of steel, about half a foot long, so fine at the point as to bend at the first hit, so that when thrown against an enemy it could not be used again, otherwise it would serve both parties, and he that lanceth would provide weapons for his adversary to annoy him."

The funditores, or slingers, were generally from the Balearic isles, or Achæans.[1] Several of these may be seen on the Trajan column, and there appear in tunics with only a helmet and shield to protect them; the shape of the sling seems in those specimens of the ordinary kind, and Mezentius, on the 9th Æneid[2] of Virgil, has observed, that, before it was loosened from the hand, it was whirled three times round the head:

> Ipse ter adducta circum caput egit habena.
>
> "Thrice round his head the loaded sling he whirled."

And Ovid:[3]

> . . . . . Quàm cùm Balearica plumbum
> Funda jacit, volat illud, et incandescit eundo.
>
> ". . . . . Just as when the Balearic sling
> Hurls out the lead, it flies, and grows warm in its course."

From which we further learn, that these people introduced the leaden bullet into the Roman army.[4]

The Sagittarii, or archers, attached to the legion, were of various nations, but chiefly from Crete and Arabia.[5] The arrows that they used had not only their piles barbed, but were furnished with hooks just above, which easily entered the flesh, but tore it when attempted to be withdrawn; hence, Ovid[6] says,

> Et manus hamatis utraque est armata sagittis.
>
> "And his hand is armed with arrows hooked on both sides."

And Statius,

> Aspera tergeminis acies se condidit uncis.
>
> "The sharp head, with three twin hooks armed buried itself in its body."

Accius speaks of the bow-string, as made of horse intestines, thus,

> Reciproca tendens nervo equino concita
> Tela.
>
> "Drawing the arrows with an horse's nerve
> They reciprocally spring forward."

The mode of drawing the bow-string was with the fore-finger and the thumb, as depicted in representations of Amazons, on fictile vases, for Seneca, in his Hippolitus, says,

> Amentum digitis tende prioribus,
> Et totis jaculum dirige viribus.
>
> "The thong with your fore-finger draw,
> Then shoot with all your strength."

These light troops sometimes, instead of the galea, wore on their heads the galerus, which was made of the skin of a wild beast to appear more terrible. The musicians and standard-bearers are represented with such on the Trajan column, from which we learn, that it consisted of the head and mane of the animal. Polybius, however, says, that the velites had, on the tops of their casques, merely a wolf's paw, that their leaders might distinguish them.

The cavalry at first used only their ordinary clothing for the sake of agility, that they might more easily mount their horses, stirrups being neither mentioned by the classic writers, nor appearing on

[1] Liv. Lib. XXI. c. 21: XXVIII. c. 37; XXXVIII. 21, 29. [2] V. 587. [3] Metam. Lib. II. v. 727.

[4] This passage, and what has been said in the description of the Greek weapons, shews the high antiquity of the bullet. In the middle ages it was used for the cross-bow, and in later times for the musket.

[5] Livy, XXXVIII. 40: XLII. 35. [6] De Amore.

antient coins and statues. When these were first used is uncertain, but their Latin name is stapedæ, or stapiæ, "stations for the feet." Neither the Greeks nor Romans had what may properly be called saddles, but either the skins of wild animals, or some drapery, termed by the former ephippia, and by the latter vestis stragula, were put on the horse's back :[1] these were kept in their places by a breast-band and a breeching, and from whence they issued were little loops, to which the warrior, when dismounted, affixed his shield.[2] The saddle, however, had been adopted in the time of Theodosius, as may be observed on the column of that emperor, and its form is delineated in Pl. LXXX, Fig. 1, of this work.

Polybius, describing the Roman cavalry nearly a century and a half before the Christian æra, says, "Their armour is now the same as that used by the Greeks, formerly, however, they did not wear loricæ, but only had coverings for their thighs, which rendered them lighter, and more readily able to dismount, though fighting thus without armour they were more exposed to danger. Their javelins were useless weapons for two reasons, first, because they were so slender as to bend with their own weight, and hence sometimes broken by the motion of the horse ; and next, because being armed with iron at one end only, they were merely suited for one thrust, which broke and rendered them unserviceable. They carried too, a buckler made of the hide of an ox, which resembled loaves indented,[3] such as are used at sacrifices ; and these not being firm enough to make any resistance were of little use at best, but when thoroughly wet with rain quite unserviceable. It was on this account, that, after the submission of Greece, they laid aside all those things, and adopted the Greek arms instead, by which they are now able to secure the blow, the javelin being firm, and capable of being used at either end."[4]

In consequence of this change of the armour and weapons, Pliny at a latter period, wrote a book de jaculatione equestri,[5] or the art of using the javelin on horseback, but which, unfortunately, has not come down to us. When the cavalry, like that of the Greeks, wore armour similar to the infantry,[6] they were called loricati, but long after this period the major part consisted of light troops. So early however as the days of Livy, there was a body of heavy horse, termed equites cataphracti, which seem to have been borrowed from the eastern nations through the medium of the Greeks.[7]

Sallust, in a fragment preserved by Servius an antient scholiast on Virgil, explains the equites cataphracti thus, "ferreâ omni specie equis paria operimenta, quæ linteo ferreis laminis in modum plumæ adnexuerunt," "they were clad in steel, their horses were in similar armour made of linen, with laminæ of iron fastened on them, in the manner that feathers overlap each other in a plume :" on which Servius observes, Pluma est in armaturâ, ubi lamina in laminam se indit, "the plume in armour is where one lamina is placed over the other." This similitude to plumes of feathers, Justin and others consider as resembling the scales of fish, whence they were denominated loricæ squammatæ. The appearance differs but slightly, the mode of attaching them not at all. Virgil in the passage commented on by Servius, towards the end of the 11th book[8] of the Æneid, unites the similitude of both, but describing the material as brass, and the laminæ fastened on leather instead of linen,

Spumantemque agitabat equum, quem pellis ahenis
In plumam squammis auro conserta tegebat.

"And drove on the foaming horse, whom a skin,
Covered with brazen scales, like feathers, and thick-set with gold, protected."

Quintus Curtius speaks of this kind of armour, though he does not distinguish whether the pieces of iron were shaped like scales, or quadrangular laminæ. He says, "equitibus, equisque tegumenta erant ex ferreis laminis seriè inter se connexis." "The armour of the Asiatic horses and their riders

[1] Horat. Epist. I. 14. 44; Liv. XXI. 54. [2] Several specimens occur on the Trajan column. [3] Concave.

[4] Polyb. Liv. VI. The Stradiots, or Greek troops, anciently in the pay of France, used similar javelins. For one of these see Plate IV. Fig. 4. [5] Plin. Ep. III. 4.

[6] Josephus, Lib. III. Excidii Ierosolym. says, Galeas et loricas omnes habeant, uti pedites.

[7] Lib. XXXV. 48; XXXVII. 40. [8] V. 770. [9] Lib. IV.

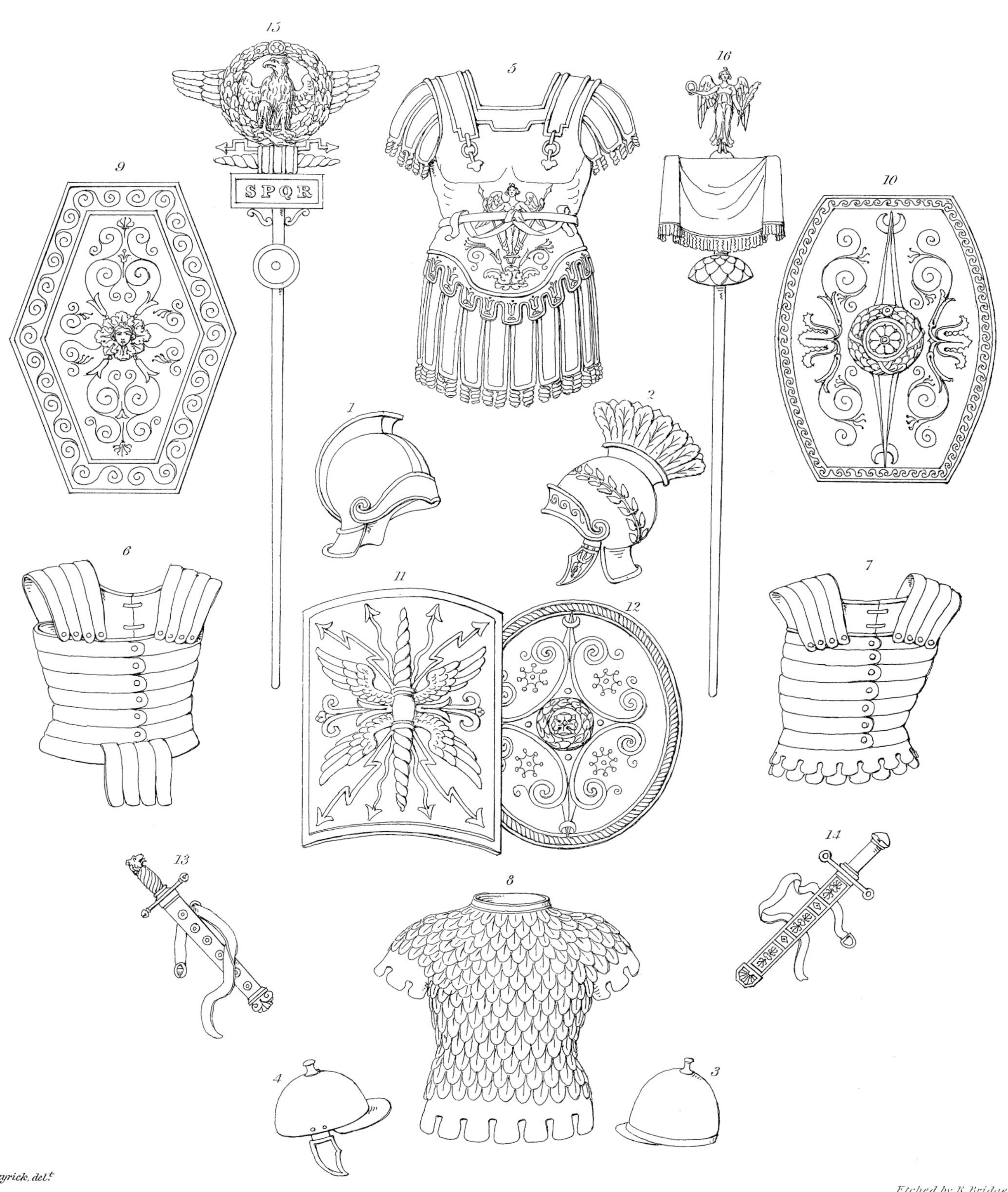

S. R. Meyrick, del.t

Etched by R. Bridgens.

ROMAN ARMOUR.

was of iron laminæ, connected in rows one with another." Ammianus Marcellinus[1] tells us, that in the time of Constantine the Great the cataphracti equites composed part of the Roman army; and adds, they were the same as the Persians called clibanarii. He says, thoracum muniti tegminibus et limbis ferreis cincti, ut Praxitelis manu polita crederes simulacra, non viros, quos laminarum circuli tenues apti corporis flexibus ambiebant per omnia membra deducti, ut quocunque artus necessitas commovisset, vestitus congrueret junctura cohærenter aptata. "They were protected with armour, in the form of thoraces, and girt with bands of iron, so that you might rather have supposed them statues formed by the hand of Praxiteles, than men who were enveloped with thin rings of laminæ,[2] so fitted to the movements of their bodies, and brought over all their members, that in whatever direction occasion required the limbs to move, the adhering and closely fitted covering followed the movement."

Lampridius also says they were the same as the Persian clibanarii. From Nazarius we learn, that armour made after this fashion was called operimentum ferri.[3] In his Panegyric he asks, "What is said to have been that species so dreadful to behold, so terrible? Horses and men covered in steel work. It is called in the army clibanarium. Above the breasts of the horses, which are entirely covered, the lorica[4] hangs down and reaches as far as the thighs, they can proceed without impediment, it protects them from the injury of wounds." These troops Trebellius, in Claudio and in Alexandro Severo, says, were commonly called cataphracti, or cataphractarii. Claudian, in the sixth consulship of Honorius, elegantly speaks of steel armour, and probably the scaled. His words are,

Ut chalybe indutos equites, et in æra latentes
Vidit cornipedes. Quânam de gente rogabat
Ferrati venêre viri? Quæ terra metallo
Nascentes informat equos? Num Lemnius auctor
Addidit hinnitum ferro, simulacraque bellis
Viva dedit?

"When he saw the steel-clad horsemen, and the hard hoofed steeds,
Covered with brass. From what nation, he asked,
Have these iron-clad men come? What land gives birth
To horses clothed in metal? Was Lemnius[5] the inventor,
Who has given to iron the power of neighing, and sent to the wars
Animated images?"

Here, though the material is named, the form of the armour is by no means specified, but its fashion may be gathered from what he says elsewhere,[6] where he speaks of little plates sewn together:

Flexilis inductis hamatur lamina[7] membris,
Horribilis visu: credat simulacra moveri
Ferrea, cognatoque, viros spirare metallo.
Par vestitus equis.

"The flexible lamina is hooked together, being put on his limbs,
Horrible to the sight: you might believe him to be a moving
Image of iron, and that men breathed from the kindred metal.
The horse is clad in the same manner."

Vegetius does not seem to approve of this kind of heavy cavalry; he says, "the equites cataphracti, on account of the armour which they wear, are secure from wounds, but its inconvenience and weight render them liable to be easily taken prisoners." The troops, however, thus accoutred,

1 Lib. XVI.

2 This seems to refer to the flat-ringed or the rustred armour, or rather, that the scales were held by little rings. See this subject amply discussed in a paper in the 19th volume of the Archæologia.

3 Or munimenta, tegumenta, and tegmina loricæ.

4 It here implies the armour for the horse.

5 Vulcan.

6 Lib. II. in Rufinum.

7 The hamata lamina in this sentence seems to be the same as the laminarum circuli of Ammianus.

were not Romans, but foreigners levied in the subdued provinces, who were armed in their national manner: hence, we find that the equites cataphracti have always attached to them, in the Notitia, the epithets Persæ, Palmirenorum, Parthi, Ambianenses, &c.

Cæsar[1] says, that in his time, "almost all the knights had tunics or armour (tegmenta), either of stuffed or quilted work (subcoacta), or tanned garments (centones), by which they secured themselves from the weapons aimed at them." Pliny[2] explains this more particularly by saying that the garment thus made was stuffed with wool only.

In all this there is nothing like plate armour, except the breast and back plates in the British Museum: but the antients, nevertheless, used a plate for the horses' forehead, called a frontal. Euripides describes this as solid when he speaks of Rhæsus and his horses:

> "A shield on his shoulder shone, with
> Golden figures united. But the Gorgon,
> Such as is on the shield of Pallas, was of iron,
> And strapped to the foreheads of the horses."

At a latter period the emperor Leo says,[3] "the horses, especially those of the præfects, should have pectorals and frontals, either made of iron, of prepared hides, or of sinews, on their breasts and necks, if that can be done; and their bodies should be protected by small pieces suspended from the feletra of their saddles, which would preserve from the greatest dangers both horses and riders. The antients armed their horses with laterals and frontals." In the next section he says, "others of the equites cataphracti had contaria, that is, spears, which were formerly called lonchæ, but now menaula, and these are of service in a charge. Others, who throw their weapons from a distance, are called acrobolistæ, velitares, &c. Others, thureoi, because they have shields, while some again fight without, having merely lances." These thureoi are called in the Notitia Imperii, equites scutati. In section 33, Leo says, "the equites acrobolistæ, use rhectarii (peculiar kind of javelins,) others bows. Of this class too, some throw their spears from a distance, some ride up at once to attack, and others gallop round the enemy: these last are called hippocontistæ, arquites, (probably from arcus and equites,) or hippotoxotæ. Some of these are so expert in the use of their darts, that they return to the fight again and again. Of the rest some enter the conflict with spears, swift-flying darts, or swords; and these are the velites, or light cavalry: some of them carry small battle axes, and in such manner the antients organized their bodies of cavalry." In confirmation of this, it may be here mentioned, that Cæsar and Hirtius,[4] speak of mounted archers, whom they call hippotoxotæ.

From various passages of the classic authors we may collect, that the antients not only greatly esteemed white or grey horses, but preferred them, from an idea that they excelled in swiftness those of a different colour.

> Qui candore nives anteirunt cursibus auras.
>
> "Those with the whiteness of snow will outstrip the wind in their course."

It has been observed, that the Roman cavalry were distinguished into light and heavy horse: hence Ælian, in his Tactics, says, equestres copiæ modo armaturæ inter se distant, pars enim tota obsepta est, et hinc cataphracti, pars non tota armis tegitur. Cataphractos igitur eos intelligi volo, qui non solum sua corpora, sed etiam equos loricâ undique muniunt. The light cavalry wore leathern loricæ, or tunics stuffed with wool, &c. hence, Varro says, "they make their pectorals de 'corio crudo' of raw hides;" and Pliny,[5] "they make a garment which they stuff with wool, and if to this vinegar be added it will even resist steel." Such cuirasses, however, were edged with iron round the neck, and sometimes round the line of the abdomen. Hence, Silius Italicus[6] says,

> . . . . Ferro circumdare pectus.
>
> " . . . . To surround the breast with iron."

[1] Lib. III. of his History of the Civil Wars. [2] Lib. VIII. c. xlviii. [3] In his Tactics, cvi. s. 8. and s. 31.
[4] De Bello Civ. Lib. III. Hirtius de Bello Africano. [5] Lib. VIII. c. 48. [6] Lib. VIII.

The Greek cavalry in the service of Rome, at the destruction of Jerusalem, are described by Josephus, as having a long sword suspended at their right side, a long contum in their hand, three or four javelins with broad heads in a quiver, and a ponderous spear. In the light cavalry were included equites sagittarii, as well as jaculatores equites.

That the Romans used spurs is evident from the discovery of two at Woodchester, of the spear-kind, but without a neck.[1] They are of iron, which was frequently the case, as appears from many passages in the Roman writers. Virgil says,[2]

Quadrupedemque citum ferratâ calce fatigat.

"And he fatigues the swift quadruped with the iron spur."

Silius Italicus has the same expression.[3] But they have been found of brass. A particular sharp bit was sometimes used, called lupus or lupatum, the wolf or wolfish, but from what cause the learned are not agreed.[4] Hence Horace[5] says

.... Gallica nec lupatis
Temperet ora frænis.

"........ Nor with wolfed bits
Manage the mouth of the Gallic horse."

The ordinary bit, however, was merely a thin bar of iron, with large rings at its extremities. Such an one, found near Frome, in Somersetshire, was presented by B. E. Willoughby, Esq., to the armoury at Goodrich Court.

It was not only the practice of the Greeks and Spaniards to have their horses taught submissively to stoop and take their riders on their backs, but that of the Romans as appears in their early history. Hence Silius Italicus,[6] speaking of the horse of Clælius, a Roman knight, says,

Inde inclinatus collum, submissus et armos
De more, inflexis prædebat scandere terga
Cruribus.

"Downwards the horse his head and shoulders bent,
To give his rider a more free ascent."

The Romans at one time used elephants in their armies, and Cæsar sent one into Britain, which, we are told by Polyænus,[7] was mailed in scales of iron, with a tower on its back, in which were archers and slingers. This quadruped easily put the terrified Britons to flight.

These animals had their foreheads protected by a large plate, in which was fixed a spike,[8] a fashion retained in India at the present time. On a Roman coin,[9] the armour of the elephants appears to consist of a trellis-work, probably of leather, and this occurs again on one of the tessellated pavements, discovered at Woodchester, in Gloucestershire:[10] only that part of the head from the eyes to the tip of the trunk being without it. In the coin alluded to, a naked man, with three darts in his hand, is represented sitting on the elephant's back.

In this review of the Roman armour we have seen nothing like interlaced rings, or double chain-mail, still hooks and chains are mentioned, and it therefore remains to inquire what was meant by these words, Statius, in his Thebaid,[11] says,

1 See Lysons' Woodchester Antiq. xxxv. 2 Æn. xi. v. 714. 3 Lib. viii. 696.

4 By Servius' comment on Virg. 3. Georg. v. 208, it would appear that the lupus was so called, from its having unequal jags like the teeth of a wolf. In the Doucean Museum at Goodrich Court is what I conceive to be the centre part of one of these bits, of bronze. It consists of three spikes, about an inch long, placed upright, two in front and one behind, upon a base, to each end of which is a fixed ring, to which was attached the remainder of the bit. It would lie flat in the horse's mouth until checked, when rising, it would instantly take effect. 5 Lib. i, Od. viii.

6 Lib. x. 7 In his stratagems. 8 Livy, Lib. xxxvii.

9 Superscribed Æternitas Augg. in Montfaucon's Antiq. expl. Vol. I. p. 334. The elephants appear the same on a diptick of the Consul Basilius, given by Montf. Sup. Vol. III. Pl. lxxx.

10 See Lysons' publication on that subject. 11 Lib. vii.

.... Ter insuto servant ingentia ferro
Pectora.

"........ With triple plates of iron they defend
Their breasts."

And from another passage,[1] we learn in what manner these plates were kept together :

Multiplicem tenues iterant thoraca catenæ,

"The little chains join the many-folded thorax."

Hence the chain-work does not appear to have of itself made the armour, but merely to have been an accessory to it; the hooks were for the same purpose. Virgil says,[2]

Loricam consertam hamis, auroque trilicem.

"The three-fold lorica held together with golden hooks."

Which is still more clearly explained by Silius Italicus. Speaking of the Consul Flaminius, he says,[3]

Loricam induitur tortos huic nexilis hamos
Ferro squamma rudi, permistoque asperat auro.

"He puts on the lorica, it looks terrible: scales
Of plain iron and gold intermixed,
Being knitted together with the twisted hooks."[4]

From all these quotations it appears, that the hooks and chains were merely employed as auxiliary.

As the Roman armour was generally of brass, so were their weapons of steel.[5] They had, indeed, in their infant state, used brazen weapons, and many discoveries in Italy seem to prove this, but from their arrival in Britain, the writings of their authors and repeated exhumations prove iron to have been the general material.[6] The hilts of the swords were of brass or copper, even when the blades came to be made of steel.[7]

At Woodchester was discovered a dagger near a foot long, and much resembling a modern French bayonet-blade, the ferrule of a scabbard, a barbed arrow-head, and a sword-blade, resembling a large broad knife, all of iron, and of undoubted Roman origin.[8] Mr. Douglas, in his Nenia Britannica, gives an engraving of a Roman gladius of iron, found with a fibula of brass, the blade of which is nineteen inches and a half long. Cæsar encouraged his men, according to Polyænus,[10] to have their arms richly ornamented with gold and silver, in order to make their owners more reluctantly part with them.

The Roman officers wore a military cloak, which was called paludamentum,[11] and very similar to the chlamys of the Greeks; it was of a scarlet colour, bordered with purple. Under this they sometimes wore a tunic, called sagum, said to have been borrowed from the Gauls. This, Polyænus tells us, was introduced by Scipio, who used himself to wear one of black.[12]

[1] Theb. XII. [2] Æn. III, v. 467. [3] Lib. V.

[4] The hooks, or rather, as we have seen, the rings, divided in one place, were used for holding together the scales, and, therefore, might have helped to compose a garment wholly of metal. But if the interlaced ringed armour was known to the antients, how did it happen that it was forgotten in Europe till the 13th century? Piranesi's engravings of the sculptures on the Trajan Column, representing the spoils of the Dacians and Sarmatians, exhibit short-sleeved hauberks of interlaced mail, and head-pieces with a sort of camail, or defence for the neck appended to them, of the same mail, which is represented precisely in the same manner as the interlaced mail on Effiges of the 14th and 15th centuries. The authority of Piranesi alone may be called in question, as no similar representations have elsewhere occurred, but the fact is one that well deserves to be verified by a careful examination of the original.

[5] Yet Tacitus, Hist. Lib. II, mentions Otho as wearing an iron breast-plate to shew his humility.

[6] General Melvill was also of this opinion. See Archæologia, Vol. VII, p. 374.

[7] Brazen swords or daggers, with hilts and sheaths of the same material, may be seen in the British Museum.

[8] See Lysons' Woodchester Antiquities, Pl. XXXV.

[9] Pl. XXVI. The same is noticed in Archæologia, Vol. VII, p. 375. [10] Lib. VIII, c. 23.

[11] Lib. I, c. 26; Plin. XVI, 3; Tacit. Ann. Lib. XII, c. 56; and Juvenal's Sat. VI, 399. [12] Lib. VIII, c. XV.

From Vegetius[1] we learn, that a centurion was chosen, whose office it was to see that all the arms of the infantry were in proper order, sharpened, and kept bright; in the same manner a decurion, who commanded a troop of cavalry, had to attend to his men, whether loricati or cataphracti, to see that they took care of and frequently cleaned their armour, as well as their conti and helmets; and Vegetius observes that the splendour of arms adds considerably to the terror of an enemy."

There were certain soldiers appointed under a prefect, to act as city watch-guards, of which there were seven cohorts, one for every two wards. They were composed chiefly of manumitted slaves, and wore over their tunics three leathern straps, which were crossed longitudinally by three in front and three behind, and where these intersected was hung a bell.[2]

Each century, or, at least, each maniple of troops, had its proper standard and standard-bearer.[3] This was originally merely a bundle of hay on the top of a pole; afterwards a spear, with a cross piece of wood on the top, sometimes the figure of a hand above, probably in allusion to the word manipulus, and below a small round or oval shield, generally of silver[4] or of gold.[5] On this metal plate were antiently represented the warlike deities, Mars or Minerva, but after the extinction of the commonwealth the effigies of the emperors or their favourites:[6] it was on this account that the standards were called numina legionum, and held in religious veneration. The standards of different divisions had certain letters inscribed on them to distinguish the one from the other.[7] The standard of a legion, according to Dio,[8] was a silver eagle, with expanded wings, on the top of a spear, sometimes holding a thunder bolt in its claws; hence, the word aquila was used to signify a legion.[9] The place for this standard was near the general, almost in the centre. Before the time of Marius figures of other animals were used, and it was then carried in front of the first maniple of the triarii.[10] The vexillum, or flag of the cavalry, was, according to Livy, a square piece of cloth, fixed to a cross bar, on the end of a spear. The labarum, borrowed by the Greek emperors from the Celtic tribes, by whom it was called llab, was similar to this, but with the monogram of Christ worked upon it.

Vegetius[11] wonders by what fatality it happened that the Romans, after having experienced the advantage of their armour during a space of 1,200 years, from the foundation of Rome to the reign of Gratian, should at length abandon their antient discipline, and, by laying aside their breastplates and helmets, put themselves on a level with the barbarians.

Plate VI, Fig. 1, is the helmet used in the time of the republic. Fig. 2, that used in the time of the emperors. Fig. 3, is a Roman-British helmet, found in Hertfordshire, and now in the British Museum, it is of bronze. Fig. 5, is a general's lorica, with the zone tied round it. Fig. 6, a laminated cuirass worn by the private soldiers in the time of the emperors, seen in front. Fig. 7, another, seen behind. Fig. 8, a plumated lorica of the time of Trajan. Fig. 9, 10, and 11, various shaped scuta, or shields. Fig. 12, a clypeus, or buckler. Fig. 13 and 14, Roman swords. Fig. 15, the principal signum, or standard of the infantry. Fig. 16, the vexillum, or colours of the cavalry.

The Roman mode of attack and defence is very fully described by Tacitus,[12] where he relates the particulars of the siege of Cremona, in the war between Vitellius and Otho. "Antonius, the Othonian general, invested the fortified camp of the German legions, and began his attack at a distance with a volley of stones and darts. The advantage was on the side of the besieged, they possessed the heights, and with surer aim annoyed the enemy at the foot of the ramparts. Antonius saw the necessity of dividing his operations: to some of the legions he assigned distinct parts of the works, and ordered others to advance against the gates. By this mode of attack in different quarters, he knew that valour as well as cowardice would be conspicuous, and a spirit of emulation would animate the whole army.

1 Lib. II, c xxiv.

2 Suet. Aug. 25 and 30. Dio, LIV, 4. See one in Hope's Costume of the Antients.

3 Varro de Lat. Ling. IV, 16; Liv. Lib. VIII, c. viii; Veget. Lib. II, c. xxiii.

4 Plin. Lib. XXXIII, c iii.

5 Herodian, Lib. IV, c. vii.

6 Tacit. Ann. Lib. I, c. xliii; Suet. Tib. XLVIII; Cal. XIV.

7 Veget. Lib. II, c. xiii.

8 Lib. XL, c. xviii.

9 Cæs. Hisp. XXX.

10 Plin. Lib. X, c. IV, s. 5; Sallust Cat. c. LIX. Mr. Lysons, in his Reliq. Brit. Romanæ, has represented several silver laminæ and other antiquities, which he calls parts of Roman Standards, but the late Mr. Douce agreed with me in thinking that he was quite mistaken, and that some of the inscriptions on them refer to quite a different subject. They were found at Stoney Stratford, Bucks.

11 Lib. I. c. xi, s. 12.

12 Hist. Lib. III.

The third and seventh legions took their stations opposite to the road that leads to Bedriacum, the seventh and eighth Claudian legions carried on the siege on the right hand of the town, and the thirteenth invested the gate that looked towards Brixia. In this position the troops rested on their arms, till they were supplied from the neighbouring villages with pickaxes, spades, hooks, and scaling-ladders. Being at length provided, they formed a military shell with their shields, and under that cover advanced to the ramparts. The Roman art of war was seen on both sides. The Vitellians rolled down massy stones, and wherever they saw an opening, inserting their long poles and spears, rent asunder the whole frame and texture formed by the shields, while the assailants, deprived of shelter, suffered a terrible slaughter. Cremona being devoted to plunder, nothing could restrain the ardour of the soldiers. Braving wounds, danger, and death itself, they began to sap the foundation of the walls, they battered the gates, they joined their shields over their heads, and mounting on the shoulders of their comrades grappled with the besieged, and dragged them headlong from the ramparts. The most vigorous assault was made by the third and seventh legions; to support them, Antonius in person led on a select body of auxiliaries. The Vitellians were no longer able to sustain the shock, they saw their darts fall on the military shell, and glide off without effect. Enraged at this disappointment, and in a fit of despair, they hurled down their missile battering engine on the heads of the besiegers, numbers were crushed by the fall of such a ponderous mass. It happened, however, that the machine drew after it the parapet and part of the rampart; an adjoining tower, which had been incessantly battered, fell at the same time, and left a breach for the troops to enter: the seventh legion, in the form of a wedge, endeavoured to force its way, while the third hewed down the gates, and the camp was taken.

"The whole space between the camp and the walls of Cremona was one continued scene of blood. The town itself presented new difficulties, high walls and towers of stone, the gates secured by iron bars, and the works well manned with troops. Antonius ordered his men to advance with missile combustibles, and set fire to the pleasant villas that lay round the city, in hopes that the inhabitants, seeing their mansions destroyed, would more readily submit to a capitulation. In the houses that stood near the walls he placed the bravest of his troops, and from those stations large rafts of timber, stones, and firebrands, were thrown in upon the garrison. The Vitellians were no longer able to sustain their posts. The legions under Antonius were now preparing for a general assault, they formed their military shell, and advanced to the works, while the rest of the army poured in a volley of stones and darts. The besieged began to despair, and finally capitulated."

The same author thus[1] speaks of the military machines of the Romans, "some Roman deserters taught the Germans to make a kind of pluteus," or what, in subsequent ages, was called a chatfaulx. He describes it as being "a platform made of rude materials in the shape of a bridge, and constructed so as to move forward on wheels. From the top of the arch, as from a rampart, some were able to annoy the besieged, while others, under its cover, endeavoured to sap the walls. They then began to prepare pent-houses,[2] and to form a covered way with hurdles. The besieged attacked them with a volley of flaming javelins, and poured forth such an incessant fire, that the assailants were on every side enveloped by the flames."

He also tells us, that "the Romans used poles, pointed with iron, which were darted at random; nor did they discharge their massive stones without being sure of their effect. They, moreover, by hurling strong beams and other instruments crushed a strong tower, of two floors, made by the Germans, and the soldiers posted therein lay buried under the ruins. The legionary soldiers, in the mean time, framed with skill a number of new machines: one in particular struck the enemy with terror and amazement. This was so constructed, that an arm projecting from the top waved over the heads of the barbarians, till being suddenly let down, it caught hold of the combatants, and, springing back with sudden elasticity, carried them up into the air in view of the astonished Germans, and, turning round with rapidity, threw them headlong into the camp."

We learn however from Polybius,[3] that this extraordinary engine had been invented by Archimedes, and used at the siege of Syracuse.

[1] Hist. Lib. IV. [2] Called, in subsequent ages, "cats." [3] Lib. VIII.

LIGURIAN ARMOUR.

"These," says Diodorus,[1] "are a hardy race, but lighter armed than the Romans, for they defend themselves with a long shield,[2] made after the fashion of the Gauls. Their tunics are girt about them with a belt, over which they throw the skin of some wild beast: their swords are of ordinary length. From their intercourse with the Romans, however, they have mostly changed their antient mode of arming."

BALEARES.

It was not possible to speak of the Greeks, Carthaginians, and Romans, without noticing the skill of the Baleares in the use of the sling, but nothing was then said about their manner of using it. Diodorus, the Sicilian,[3] describes them more particularly. He says, their arms are three slings: one they wind about their heads, another they tie about their loins, and the third they carry in their hands. In time of war they throw much greater stones than any other people, and with as much violence as if shot from a catapulta: on this account they are called Baleares, from the Greek word βάλλειν, "to cast." Hence, when they assault a town, they grievously gall those on the bulwarks; and, in the field, break in pieces shields, helmets, and all the defensive armour of their enemies: indeed, they are such expert marksmen as scarce ever to miss their object. They are taught from their childhood; and as an incitement, their mothers place their daily food on a pole for them to aim at, and keep them fasting until they succeed in hitting it.

GAULISH ARMOUR.

Diodorus gives us[4] the following account of the Gauls, "in their fights they use chariots with a pair of horses, each holding a charioteer and a warrior, and when they engage cavalry they attack them with their barbaric weapons, called saunians, and then, quitting their cars, fall to with their swords. Many of them so despise death as to fight naked, with merely something round their loins. When a Gallic army is drawn up in order of battle, it is usual for the chiefs to step out before the line and challenge the stoutest of their enemies to single combat, brandishing their arms to terrify their adversary. They deliver their spoils to their attendants, all besmeared with blood, to be carried before them in triumph, they themselves singing the song of victory. Their defensive arms are, a shield proportionable to the height of a man, garnished with his own ensigns."[5] These, Pausanias also calls thureoi, adding, that they were introduced into Greece by Brennus. He tells us, "the Gauls had no other defence, and used them as rafts on crossing a river." This kind of shield is depicted Pl. I, Fig. 5. That carried, however, by the Parisian boatmen, in the time of Tiberius Cæsar, and of which a sculptured representation was found in Paris, at Notre Dame, in 1711, appears to be hexagonal and convex, though long and narrow.[6] Diodorus says further, "some of the Gauls carry the shapes of beasts in brass, artificially wrought, as well for defence as ornament.[7] Upon their heads they wear helmets of brass, with large appendages for the sake of ostentation, for they have either horns of the same metal joined to them, or the shapes of birds and beasts. They have trumpets[8] after the barbarian manner, which, when sounded, make a dreadful noise. Some of them wear iron thoraces, and hooked;[9] but others, content with what nature affords them, fight naked. They wear bracelets on

1 Lib. v. c. ii.
2 Παραμήκης θυρεὸς.
3 Lib. v, c. i.
4 Lib. v, c. ii.
5 Θυρεοῖς μὲν ανδρομήκεσι πεποικιλμένοις ἰδιοτρόπως.
6 See Montfaucon's Antiq. expl. Vol. II, p. 423.
7 Whether these were used as shields or body-armour does not appear from the context.
8 See an Irish one of a similar kind called buadhvail, or the mouth-piece of Victory, in the Costume of the original inhabitants of the British Isles.
9 Θώρακας σιδηροῦς ἁλυσιδωτοὺς.

their arms and wrists of pure gold, torques round their necks of the same metal, and rings of gold on their fingers ; golden thoraces are sometimes worn." As Diodorus does not mention these latter when enumerating the arms and armour of the Gauls, they might probably be used as ornaments by the judges, and the same as the jodhain moran of gold, frequently found in Ireland. Yet the discovery of a golden thorax in North Wales, now in the British Museum, and engraved in the Archæologia, rather tends to class it with armour. Those with the hooked cuirasses are probably the same as Tacitus calls[1] crupellarii, "whose armour," he says, "rendered them less efficient for inflicting wounds but impenetrable to receiving them." "For swords," Diodorus adds, "they used a long and broad weapon called spatha, which they suspended by iron or brazen chains on their right thigh ;" and Posidonius mentions that "they carried a dagger which served the purpose of a knife."[2] Diodorus says, "for darts they cast those called lankia, whose iron blades are a cubit or more in length, and almost two hands in breadth." Propertius attributes to them one of a particular kind, which he calls gesum. Hence, speaking of Viridumarus, he says,

> Nobilis é tectis fundere gesa rota.
>
> "Nobly standing on the roofs to hurl down the whirling gesa."

"Though their swords are as large as the saunians of other nations, the points of their saunians are larger than those of their swords : some of them are straight, others bowed or bending backwards, so that they not only cut but break the flesh, and when the dart is drawn out, it tears and rends the wound most exceedingly."

Some of the Gauls were exhibited in the games at Rome as gladiators, and from the shapes of animals, which Diodorus notices, on their helmets, derived their name.[3] The first who exhibited had chosen a fish for their crest, whence they were called mirmillones, from the Greek *μορμυρος*, a fish : and this designation was probably given by their adversaries, who were Thracians. The mirmillo was armed with a small circular shield, and a curved sword, the edge of which was inside.[4]

CELTIBERIAN ARMOUR.

"These people," says Diodorus the Sicilian,[5] "bring into the field not only stout and valiant horsemen, but brave infantry, strong, hardy, and able to undergo all kind of labour and toil. Some of them are armed with shields resembling the light ones of the Gauls ; others with curtiæ or bucklers, as large as shields.[6] They wear on their legs greaves made of rough hair, and on their heads helmets of brass adorned with red plumes. They carry two-edged swords of well-tempered steel, and have besides daggers a span long, of which they make use in close fights. They make weapons and darts in an admirable manner, for they bury plates of iron so long under ground as is necessary for the rust to consume the weaker part, and therefore use only that which is strong and firm. Swords and other weapons are made of this prepared steel, and these arms are so powerful in cutting, that neither shield, helmet, nor bone can withstand them. As they are furnished with two swords, the cavalry, when they have routed their antagonists, dismount, and, joining the infantry, fight as auxiliaries." Strabo tells us, that it was the practice of the Spaniards to teach their horses to stoop and take their riders on their backs.[7]

[1] Crupellarii continuo ferri tegmine inferendis ictibus inhabites dolabris et securibus à Romanis cœduntur. Lib. xx.

[2] "In Athenæus, Lib. xiv.

[3] Hence, according to Festus a retiarius called out, "Non te peto, piscem puto quid me fugis Galle ?"

[4] Gladio incurvo et falcato. On a lamp, engraved in Montf. Antiq. expl. Tom. V, Pl. cxcvi, is such a combat, in which the curved sword, with the device of a snake on the helmet are fully visible : the shield, however, used by the mirmillo is oblong.

[5] Lib. v. c. ii.

[6] Κυρτίαις κυκλοτέρεσιν, ἀσπίδων ἐχούσαις τὰ μεγέθη. Lucan, Lib. i, says the Spaniards used a small shield, called Cetra, which a part of the Roman cavalry afterwards adopting, were termed, in the Notitia Imperii, cetrati equites.

[7] Lib. iii.

LUSITANIAN ARMOUR.

Diodorus says,[1] "those who are called Lusitanians are the most valiant of all the Cimbri. In time of war they carry little targets[2] made of bowel-strings, so strong and firm as completely to guard and defend their bodies: they manage them with such dexterity, that by whirling them about here and there with skill, they avoid or repel every dart thrown at them. They use hooked[3] saunians, made all of iron, and wear swords and helmets like those of the Celtiberians. They throw their darts at a great distance, and yet are sure to hit their mark and wound deeply. Being active and nimble they easily pursue or retreat from an enemy, but they cannot bear hardships so well as the Celtiberians."

GERMAN ARMOUR.

Tacitus describes[4] the Germans who lived near the Weser as "wearing neither helmets nor breastplates, but armed with a spear of enormous length, and an unwieldy buckler, not rivetted with iron, nor covered with hides, but formed of osier twigs intertwined, or slight boards daubed over with glaring colours. The foremost ranks were provided with pikes and javelins, but the remainder had merely stakes hardened in the fire, or weapons too short for execution." In his account of the manners of the Germans[5] generally, he says, "Iron does not abound in Germany, if we may judge from the weapons in general use. Seldom are seen swords or the greater kind of lances, but they carry spears, which, in their language are called framea, with short and narrow blades of iron, yet they use these with so much dexterity, that they can fight with them from a distance as well as hand to hand. The infantry use missile weapons, of which each man carries a considerable number, but have neither helmet nor cap. Being naked, or at least not encumbered by his light mantle, he throws his weapon to a distance almost incredible. Their cavalry use the framea and a large shield, and these shields are distinguished by splendid colours: they are, indeed, the only objects of their care, as a German pays no attention to the ornament of his person. The infantry used these shields."

"Breastplates are uncommon, in the whole army you will not see more than one or two helmets. According to the best estimate, the infantry form the national strength, and for that reason always fight intermixed with the cavalry. Their order of battle is generally in the form of a wedge. They make it a point to carry off their slain, and hold it a flagitious crime to abandon their shields. The tribe called Cattians never rush to battle, but march to war. Each soldier carries, besides his arms, his provisions and military tools. The Arians study to make themselves horrible by every addition art can devise: their shields are black, their bodies painted of a deep colour, and the darkest night is the time for rushing to battle. The sudden surprise and funereal gloom of such a band of sable warriors are sure to strike a panic through the adverse army, who fly the field as if a legion of demons had broken loose to attack them, so true is it that in every engagement the eye is first conquered. The Rugians and Lemovians (who lived on the Baltic, near Dantzic,) use round shields and short swords. The Æstians (who inhabited Prussia) have a club as their general weapon. The Venedians know the use of shields, but the Fennians point their arrows simply with bone."

In 1053, the German infantry fought with two-handed swords, (retained for four hundred years after by the Switzers,) and were considered so strong and impenetrable a phalanx, that neither man, steed, nor armour could resist their blows. The Germans were not, however, at that time skilful in the management of the horse and lance, but this remark is only applicable to the Frankish settlers in that country.

1 Lib. v. c. ii.

2 Πέλτας μικρὰς.

3 Ἀγκιστρώδεσι.

4 Ann. Lib. II.

5 Ch. VI.

ABELLA.

VIRGIL describes[1] the inhabitants of Abella, one of the tribes of Italy, that assembled under Turnus, as having swords and circular shields of brass. This mountain tribe retained the customs of the ancient Teutones, had helmets of cork, and used the cateia, which has been supposed to be both a harpoon and a sling, but which seems to have been the same as the British cat, a club with a thong to it.

> Et quos maliferæ despectant moenia Abellæ
> Teutonico ritu soliti torquere cateias;
> Tegmina quis capitum raptus de subere cortex,
> Æratæque micant peltæ, micat æreus ensis.

> "And those on whom the walls of the applebearing Abella look,
> Accustomed to twirl the cateiæ, in the Teutonic manner,
> For the coverings of whose heads, the bark is stripped from the cork tree ;
> And whose brass-bound peltæ shine, and whose brazen swords glitter."

HUNS.

THE Huns, in the time of Valentinian, according to Zosimus, were mounted archers and very expert horsemen. Their costume may be seen on the sculptures engraved in Professor Pallas's Travels,[2] from which it appears to have resembled that of the modern Tartars.

VANDALS.

PLINY[3] and Procopius[4] coincide in opinion, that the Vandals and Goths were originally one people, and this seems to be countenanced by a similarity of manners. They were distinguished into Heruli, Burgundians, Lombards, and other petty states. They used, like the Goths, round bucklers and short swords, which rendered them formidable in a close engagement, and their forces consisted of infantry and cavalry.

SCANDINAVIAN ARMOUR.

UNDER the name of Scandinavians are comprehended all the nations on the Western coasts of the Baltic, whom the Britons called Llychlynwys, viz., the Cimbri, with the Goths and Saxons, the descendants of the Sacæ and Massa-Getæ of the Caspian, and the Danes.

The Cimbri were the most antient of these as settlers on the Baltic, and while they continued independent and distinct, seem to have worn armour, for they are represented on their invasion of Gaul as wearing iron breastplates, and carrying white shields.[5] They bore, as offensive weapons, maces, darts, and swords of unusual forms, and, according to Plutarch, had long swords, but were ignorant of the use of the helmet. The sword which Plutarch mentions seems to have been the degan or spad, so highly prized, as to be sometimes on account of its cruciform shape, the symbol of the deity. It was sharp, and often inscribed with Runic characters; and in order to create greater terror, those of the chiefs had proper names.[6] Their women, as was the case with their Gaulish and British consanguinei, fought with lances.[7]

[1] Æneid, VII. 740.
[2] Vol. I. p. 445.
[3] Hist. Nat. Lib. IV, c. 14.
[4] Bell. Vandal, Lib. I. c. i.
[5] Freinshemii Sup. in Livii, Lib. LXVIII. c. lxii.
[6] Mallet's Introd. to Hist. of Denmark.
[7] Freinshemius ut supra.

The Gothic and Sclavonian nations, who had intermixed on the western coasts of the Baltic, fought in remote periods, almost destitute of armour, a practice which from prejudice they retained long after they became familiarized with the warlike manners of their more polished neighbours.

At a later period the Saxons and Danes made use of battle-axes, bows, and arrows, and were distinguished by short curved swords slung in a belt across the right shoulder; this distinctive weapon was called saex, and its form was that of a scythe.[1] It seems to have been peculiar to the Saxons, and possibly, because fighting more constantly on horseback than the Danes, they made this weapon serve both for action and procuring fodder. The battle-axe was double-edged, that is a bipennis, and denominated byl : when these were affixed to long staves, which was generally the case for the infantry, they were termed alle-bardes, or cleave-alls.

In the most antient chronicles, the Scandinavians are represented as excellent archers, a quality for which the Anglo-Saxons do not appear to have been conspicuous. All the Northern nations made occasional use of the dart, the sling, the mace armed with points, the hammer, which was often of flint, and called Miölner,[2] the lance, and the poignard. For defence they had shields, some of which were of a long oval form, so as entirely to cover the bearer, and called skiold, whence our English world shield; others were round, but not so large, convex, and often furnished with a boss of iron or other metal.[3] The larger sort were invariably of wood, bark, or leather; the others, and particularly those of the chiefs were of iron or brass, and engraved, painted, or gilt, and sometimes covered with a plate of gold. The large shield served as a bier for the wounded, or, in the manner of the Gauls, to enable its owner to swim across a river: they were white until the bearer, by some exploit, obtained permission to bear some distinctive mark. The helmet, though often disregarded, was known to the Scandinavian and Gothic tribes, from their intercourse with the Romans, the inferior warriors wearing them of leather, and the chiefs of iron or metal gilt. The lorica they also acquired from the Romans, and if the scale-armour was not likewise borrowed from them, it might have been derived from the Sarmatians, who settled near the Baltic after the Vandals had departed. As Sweden produced the best iron in Europe, and in the greatest abundance, it will account for the arms of the northern nations being of that metal, and also so broad and heavy. The torque was an ornament of the northern warrior.

ANGLO-SAXON ARMOUR.

The Anglo-Saxons, under Hengist and other followers, wore many of them the loricæ of leather, and four-cornered helmets.[5] This armour was probably acquired through the alliance of their fathers with the Romans, under Carausius and his successors; subsequent intercourse with the Greek Emperors[6] induced them to adopt the Phrygian tunic covered with flat rings.[7] This, however, does not occur till the middle of the eighth century, about 300 years after their arrival in England. According to Aneurin, Hengist wore scale armour, and, it seems, a mantle of fur, and was armed with a large piercing weapon, and a shield made of split wood. A very early illuminated MS. in the British Museum,[8] represents a warrior exactly answering this description, his four-cornered helmet has a

1 It was also called sais, which, in the modern dialect of Lower Saxony, still signifies that implement of husbandry.

2 One of these, of compact stone, is in the armoury at Goodrich Court.

3 Many of these, as well as iron bow braces or grasps, have been found in barrows in England. See Douglas's Nenia Brit. Pl. III, and VII. One discovered in Lincolnshire is in the collection at Goodrich Court.

4 The helmet, as worn by the warriors on a golden horn found at Galhuus, in Denmark, is of the basin kind, with a nasal, and having two long feathers rising from it in the Tartar fashion.

5 Aneurin, the British bard, in his Gododins, asserts this frequently.

6 Douglas's Nenia Brit.; Gibbon's Dec. of Rom. Emp.; and Turner's Angl. Saxons.

7 Compare an illumination in a MS. in the Cotton library, marked Cleopatra, C. VIII. with the Phrygian warrior of bronze, in Hope's Costume of the Antients, before noticed.

8 In the Harl. library, No. 603.

serrated crest,[1] his spear is broad bladed, and his shield convex, with an iron boss terminating in a button, exactly like those found in the tumuli opened by the Rev. Mr. Douglas, and which are generally accompanied with a sword and dagger of steel of moderate size.

The lorica seems to have fallen into disuse after the conquest of England, for the illuminations of the eighth century represent the Anglo-Saxon soldier without any other defensive armour than the shield and helmet, which latter seems in general to have been nothing more than leather, and is often omitted even in representations of battles. His offensive arms are the sword and the spear.

The shape of the shield at this period is constantly oval, it is usually surrounded by a broad rim on the outside, and has a sharp boss protruding from the middle, both of metal: it was formed of wood, covered with leather. One of the laws of Æthelstan[2] prohibits the making of shields of sheep-skin, under the penalty of thirty shillings.

The helmet, as it is commonly represented in the drawings of this time, appears to have been nothing more than a cap of leather, with the fur turned outwards, but personages of rank had one of a conical form of metal and gilt.

The sword appears so large and long that it seems ill calculated for close fighting: the chief dependance of the warrior was, probably, in the vigour of his attack, or by keeping his opponent at bay with the shield, while he struck at him with his sword. The blade of the sword was iron or steel, and its hilt was ornamented or gilt. The head of the lance was sometimes barbed.

When the tunic supplanted the lorica, the Roman pectoral was still retained, and called Ꮒalſ-beaꞃh, or beoꞃᵹ, "neck-guard;" bꞃeoſꞇ-beðen "defence for the breast;" and bꞃeoſꞇ-ꞃoce "breast-plate." It may be seen on a warrior in an illumination, in Cott. MS. Tiberius, B. v, in which the resemblance to the Roman pectoral is quite manifest. The Saxon authors are by no means explicit with respect to the form or materials of the breast-guards, but the epithet applied to such as were of metal is "rigid." Others are mentioned which are said to have been "rough or shaggy," so that we may suppose these to have been formed of wool or hair.

Notwithstanding these remarks, the word lorica frequently occurs in the writings of the most antient Saxon authors, and as composed sometimes of metal. This seems to be intimated by Aldhelm, bishop of Sherborne, who lived in the latter part of the seventh century, in the ænigma contained in the following lines:

Roscida me genuit gelido de viscere tellus:
Non sum setigero lanarum vellere facta,
Licia nulla trahunt, nec garrula fila resultant,
Nec croceâ seres texunt lanugine vermes,
Nec radiis carpor, duro nec pectine pulsor;
Et tamen en! vestis vulgi sermone vocabor,
Spicula non vereor longis exempta pharetris.

"The dewy earth produced me from its congealed bowels:
I am not made from the rough fleeces of wool,
No woofs drew me, nor did the tremulous thread resound,
Nor did the yellow down of silk-worms form me,
I passed not through the shuttle, nor was I stricken with the wool-comb;
And yet behold! a vesture am I commonly called,
I fear not the darts that are drawn forth from the long quivers.

Whether this was the scaled armour, such as was worn by Hengist, or that made of flat rings in the Phrygian style, is not quite clear, but there is, in an illumination of the eighth century a king habited in a tunic covered with flat rings: and in another MS. of that period similar armour occurs.[3]

[1] Called by the Saxons Camb, or Comb.

[2] Leges Æthelstani apud Wilkins.

[3] See an illumination in the Cotton library in the British Museum, marked Claudius, B. IV. written about the time of Cædmon; and another marked Cleopatra, C. VIII.

The Saxon authors calls this Ꮭehꞃẏnᵹeꝺ bẏꞃn, or "ringed byrne." Some illuminations seem to shew, that the rings were worn edgewise,[1] and in either case the name is equally applicable. Still, the rarity of these specimens, and their use being confined to kings or principal chieftains, favours the idea that the manufacture was expensive. The Britons, however, in their frequent skirmishes with the Saxons, saw the utility of this armour, and their princes soon adopted it. They called it mael, i. e. steel, whence, probably the word mail,[2] afterwards so generally used as contra-distinguished from plate-armour. It is applied as an epithet to the Welsh chieftains so early as the sixth century; hence, a celebrated leader of cavalry was termed, from his wearing this armour, Mael the Tall,[3] another Maelgwyn, or "Shining Mail," Cynvael, "Mailed Chief," facts which, while they prove its existence, tend to shew its rarity.

Towards the conclusion of the ninth century the corium, or corietum, was the armour generally used, and appears frequently in the drawings of that period. It was formed of hides cut into the resemblance of leaves, covering one another, sometimes all of one colour, as blue, and sometimes of two, as brown and orange; the upper part as far as the abdomen being of the one, while that which covers the thighs is of the other colour.

It should be observed, that the Saxon byrne, originally in shape like a tunic, became in form afterwards a complete cuirass, fitting close to the body, and generally terminating with it.

Alcuin[4] speaks of the Anglo-Saxon military tunics of linen in the following terms, "the soldiers are accustomed to wear linen tunics, so well fitted to their limbs as to enable them, with the utmost expedition, to direct the dart, poise the shield, and wield the sword."

The weight of the ringed byrne seems, however, to have been found a great impediment to activity. Hence, when Earl Harold, in 1063, obtained immediate and decisive success over the Welsh, it was owing to the change of armour among his soldiers. He had observed that these mountaineers could not be pursued to their fastnesses by his troops when clad in ringed tunics, and, therefore, commanded them to use their antient leathern suits, which would not impede their agility.[5]

The Saxon artists made no distinction between the cyne-healm, or royal helmet, and the crown. The monarch is depicted by them, in his court and in the field of battle, with the same kind of head-covering even when every other part of his dress is marked with decisive variation; but upon the figure of Edward the Confessor, on his great seal, the diadem is evidently put on a helmet. The casque of the nobility is usually pointed in the form of a cone, and made of brass or some other metal. In the two succeeding centuries its shape is the same, but it is ornamented with gold and precious stones, and is improved by the addition of a small piece to protect the nose, called a nasal.[6]

Leg-guards are decidedly mentioned by the early Saxon writers, but they uniformly appear to have been made of twisted pieces of woollen cloth coming from within the shoe, and wound round the legs to the top of the calves, in imitation of the hay-bands used by their rude ancestors. The cavalry had also spurs, but do not seem ever to have adopted boots; the spur was formed on the model of the Roman, but with a much longer neck, and was called the spear-spur.

A mantle was generally worn, which was fastened on the right shoulder with a buckle; but in every contest this was laid aside.

The shield still continued oval, as indeed it did, until the Norman conquest, but it differed from time to time greatly in dimensions, especially in the tenth and eleventh centuries, in the drawings of which

[1] See an illumination in Cott. MS. Cleopatra, C. VIII.

[2] Some have derived this word from mascle, or macle, but it is of more antient use than the mascled armour.

[3] His monumental stone with its epitaph from Tregarron, Cardiganshire, is now in the ante-chapel at Goodrich Court. It is in the antient British language and the old orthography.

[4] De Offic. Divin.

[5] Ingulphus, 68; John of Salisbury de Nugis Curialium, Lib. VI. c. vi. p. 185. An author of the twelfth century also notices this invasion of Wales.

[6] See an illumination in Cott. MS. Tiberius, B. v.

times it appears of various sizes, from a magnitude sufficient to cover the head and body, to a diameter not greater than a cubit. This variation is further supported by historical testimony, for we find mention made of "little shields," and "smaller shields." In the will of Æthelstan, dated 1015, the shoulder-shield is included among the legacies, and it is distinguished from the target; it was probably of the larger sort, and received its appellation from being usually slung upon the shoulder.

The form of the sword was not subject to much variation, according to the illuminations of the period; but the Saxon records specify several sorts, as the shining sword, the sharp-pointed sword, the dull or pointless ditto, the two-edged ditto, and the broad-sword; the saex, or curved dagger, is likewise noticed. Every man of rank possessed a number of swords, suited to different occasions; upwards of a dozen, the property of Prince Æthelstan, are bequeathed in his will: and the sword-cutler appears to have been an artist held in high estimation; in antient records his name is frequently added to the arms he fabricated, as a mark of their superior excellence. Silver-hilted swords are particularly specified in the will before cited, and swords with hollow hilts. These last Mr. Strutt considers to be hilts ornamented with fret-work, and although I am by no means inclined to dispute this, I will merely mention, that in the 12th volume of the Archæologia, Pl. XLI, Fig. 4, is given the representation of a sword which belonged to a Bishop of Durham, on each side of the hilt of which is a bar, which, producing two holes for the fingers, may answer the denomination hollow-hilted.[1] Hilts of gold are also spoken of by the writers of this æra. Sometimes the sword was suspended from the shoulder, but the prevalent fashion was to gird it upon the side. The sword-belts were often not distinguished from the common girdle with which the tunic was usually bound, yet this was not always the case, and the Saxon writers speak of them as adorned with gold, silver, and jewels. The sword-sheath was generally black, but a variety of instances occur in the drawings of the time, in which they appear worn without any sheath at all.

There are three sorts of spears mentioned by Saxon authors, the war-spear, the boar-spear, and the hunting-spear, but in what respects they differed from each other cannot easily be determined. As a weapon of war it is, in drawings, given to the foot soldiers, and the cavalry are very rarely depicted without it.

To keep up the military spirit of the people their amusements were made conducive to skill in war: among these was a dance, called the sword-dance, and held in high repute, because derived from their Gothic ancestors. Tacitus, in his description of the Germans,[2] says, "one public diversion was constantly exhibited at all their meetings, young men who, by frequent exercise, have attained to great perfection in the pastime, strip themselves and dance amongst the points of swords and spears with most wonderful agility, and even with the most elegant and graceful motions. They do not perform this dance for hire, but for the entertainment of the spectators, esteeming their applause a sufficient reward." This dance continues to be practised in the Northern parts of England, about Christmas, when the foot-plough, as it is called, goes about, a pageant that consists of a number of sword-dancers dragging a plough, with music. It is, however, so far altered from its original ingenuity, that the dancers of the present day, when they have formed their swords into a figure, lay them upon the ground, and dance round them.[3] In an illuminated Saxon MS., of the ninth century,[4] a military dance of a somewhat different kind occurs: Two men, equipped in martial habits, and each armed with a sword and shield, are engaged in combat; the performance is enlivened by the sound of a horn, and the musician, together with a female assistant, dances round them to the cadence of the music, which, probably, regulated the actions of the combatants. The rapier-dance of Yorkshire seems to have been derived from this; the performers are usually dressed in a white frock, or covered with a shirt, to

[1] The three bars seem, however, to have been wholly covered by the wooden gripe. It belonged to Anthony Beck, Bishop of Durham, in 1283.

[2] De Mor. Germ. c. xxiv.

[3] See Brand's Notes upon the 14th chapter of Bourne's Vulgar Antiquities. Mr. Brand has collected, from Olaüs Magnus, the various motions and figures formed by the Gothic dancers.

[4] It is a Latin MS. of Prudentius, with Saxon Notes, in the Cotton library, marked Cleopatra, C. VIII.

which, as also to their hats or paper helmets, are suspended long black ribbons. They assume the names of military heroes, from Hector and Paris down to Guy Earl of Warwick. A spokesman repeats some verses in praise of each, when they begin to flourish their rapiers. On a signal given all the weapons are united or interlaced, but soon withdrawn again and brandished by the performers, who exhibit a great variety of evolutions, being usually accompanied by slow music: at last the rapiers are united round the neck of a person kneeling in the centre, and when they are suddenly withdrawn the victim falls to the ground. He is afterwards carried out, and a mock funeral performed.

Simeon of Durham about the year 1040, says that Earl Godwin gave to Edward the Confessor a galley having a gilded prow, manned with eighty chosen warriors armed in suitable splendour. Each wore bracelets of gold, a triple hauberk and a gilded helmet, and a sword with a gilded hilt, with a Danish axe inlaid with gold and silver were suspended at their backs. The left hand held a buckler with a gilded boss, the right a lance called in English Tegar.

Plate VII exhibits specimens of Saxon arms and armour. Fig 1 represents the large shield used at the first arrival of the Saxons, behind which are two Anglo-Saxon spears and two swords, and above it Edward the Confessor's crown-helme. Fig. 2 and 3, two specimens of the Saxon corium. Fig. 4 and 5, two helmets. Fig. 6, the antient Saxon four-cornered helmet.

In forming their armies the following regulations were observed by the Anglo-Saxons, all such as were qualified to bear arms in one family were led to the field by the head of that family. Every ten families made a tithing, which was commanded by the borsholder, in his military capacity styled conductor. Ten tithings constituted a hundred, the soldiers of which were led by their chief magistrate, called, sometimes, a hundredary: this officer was elected by the hundred, at their public court, where they met armed, and every member, as a token of his obedience to him, touched his weapon when chosen, whence the hundred courts, held for this especial purpose, were called wapen-takes, a name still retained in Yorkshire. Several hundreds were called a thrything, corrupted into riding, and this was commanded by an officer called a thrything-man, and the whole force of the county was placed under the command of the heretoch, or general. When the king did not command himself, an officer was appointed, called the kyning's-hold, or king's lieutenant, whose office lasted only during the year.

Every landholder was obliged to keep armour and weapons according to his rank and possessions; these he might neither sell, lend, nor pledge, nor even alienate from his heirs. In order to instruct them in the use of arms, they had stated times for performing their military exercise; and once in a year, usually in the spring, there was a general review of arms throughout each county.

The military affairs of Wales were regulated much in the same manner.

FRANKISH ARMOUR.

About the year 240 a new confederacy was formed against the Romans, under the name of Franks or Freemen, by the old inhabitants of the Lower Rhine and the Weser. Part of them were the Chauci, who, in their inaccessible morasses defied the Roman arms; another tribe was composed of the Cherusci, whose equipments under Arminius have been before noticed; and another class were the Catti, formidable by their firm and intrepid infantry; together with several other tribes of inferior power and renown. These united nations invaded and established themselves in Gaul, and laid the foundation of the French monarchy. As they not only spread themselves over Gaul, which they called France, but likewise great part of Germany and Italy, their name was afterwards applied, by the Greeks and Arabians, to all the Christians of the Latin church. The vast body that had been united by Charlemagne, and his wonderful victory, seems to have been the cause. A French writer of the ninth century[1] has given us a complete description of the dress of Charlemagne, who, he says, adhered strictly to all the antient manners of his country, as well in dress as every thing else. From this, we learn, that he had a military tunic of linen, exactly like those of the Anglo-Saxons, and never appeared without his sword and

[1] Eginhart de vitâ Caroli Magni, c. xxiii.

sword-belt; in these last he took particular pride. The belt was composed of gold or silver, and the hilt of the sword corresponded with the belt, except upon solemn court-days, when he wore a sword, the hilt of which was embellished with jewels. He is said, further, to have had a thorax, and in the representation given of him by Montfaucon,[1] from a mosaic of the time, this appears to have been composed of several metal plates. Excepting this thorax, there is no part of the dress of Charlemagne that may not be traced in the drawings of the Anglo-Saxons. The spurs were of the same kind, for one, in my own collection brought from Paris, of steel, though somewhat corroded, appears exactly like those in the Anglo-Saxon illuminations. But the spur shewn in Paris, as that of Charlemagne, is a pryck-spur, and nailed to the leather, whence there is reason to refer it to the 12th century. The Franks seem, however, latterly, to have imitated the Norman military habits, for in a MS. of Prudentius illuminated by the Franks, occurs the haubergeon, consisting of breeches and jacket in one, like those in the Bayeux tapestry. Some of the figures too, have, with this hauberk of the tapestry, a Saxon-crested helmet, and kite-shaped shield, while others have Saxon shields and spurs. Luitprand tells us,[2] that "the Franks were rude and unskilful in the service of cavalry; and in all perilous emergencies their warriors were so conscious of their ignorance, that they chose to dismount from their horses and fight on foot. Unpractised in the use of spears or of missile weapons, they were encumbered by the length of their swords, the weight of their armour, and by the magnitude of their shields."

Sidonius Apollinaris, who was born at Lyons about the year 460, in his Panegyric of the Emperor Majorian, gives an account of the military costume of the French under Clovis. He tells us that they were of an extraordinary height, clad in very light clothes, and wore girdles round their bodies from which their swords were suspended, that they were armed with battle-axes, and javelins, which they threw with astonishing force, never missing their object, and that they used circular shields with much address. This description would equally apply to the Anglo-Saxons. Procopius, the secretary of Belisarius, an eye-witness of the entry of the Franks into Italy under Theodobert 1st, king of Austrasian France, relates the following circumstance. "Among the 100,000 men which Theodobert led into Italy, he had a very few horsemen placed near his person, and these only carried lances, the rest of the army were infantry without bow or lance, but armed with large two-edged battle-axes, with short wooden handles, and circular shields. The manner of fighting used by these troops was varied according to the plans formed by the generals to rout the enemy, sometimes they threw the lance, and afterwards fell upon their adversaries with such alertness, as to reach them at the same time with the point of the lance which they had darted, and shattering the bucklers of their enemies, seized them, and either clave their sculls with the axe, or pierced their bodies with the sword." Their bucklers were made of twisted osier and the bark of trees, covered with very strong skin.

The scholiast Arathias, a lawyer of the sixth century, writes upon the subject as follows: "The arms of the Franks are very clumsy, they have neither armour nor protections for the legs, and few wear helmets, their cavalry is inconsiderable, but they fight on foot with great skill and discipline; they wear their sword down the thigh, and their buckler on the left side; using neither bow and arrow nor sling, but a two-edged battle-axe and javelins. The latter, which they throw, are of a moderate length and covered with iron, except at the handle; having near the point two pieces of iron bent on each side in the form of hooks, which they make use of to wound the enemy, or entangle his buckler in such a manner that his body being exposed, they run him through with their swords."

A contemporary historian, speaking of Dagobert fighting against the Saxons says, "his helmet was shattered with a blow that cut off part of his hair;" and Gregory of Tours describing the review of the troops after the battle of Soissons makes Clovis say to a soldier, "there is no one in the army whose arms are in such bad condition as yours, neither your lance, nor your sword nor double-axe are fit for service," neque tibi hasta, neque gladius neque bipennis est utilis. The same author informs us that they sometimes had a poignard hung to the girdle.

The monk of St. Gall, who wrote the life of Charlemagne, besides the helmet and hauberk, gives

[1] Monarchie Française Tom. I, Pl. XXII.

[2] In Legat. p. 480.

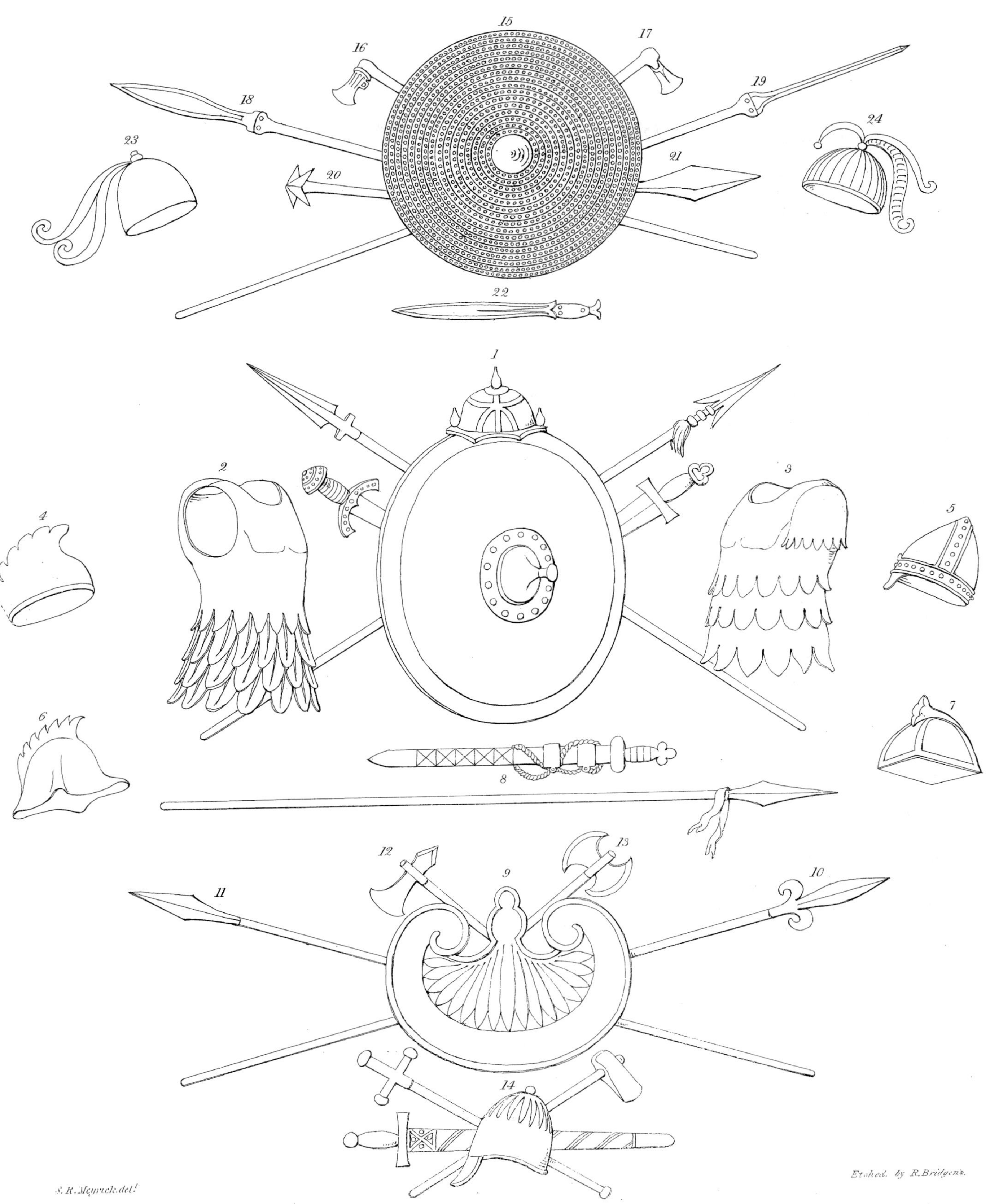

BRITISH, SAXON, AND DANISH ARMOUR.

him sleeves of mail and protections for the thighs and legs, and adds that those who accompanied him were clad after the same manner, except that in order to mount their horses the more easily they had no thigh-pieces. One of the articles of the capitularies of Charlemagne runs thus, "let the Count take care that arms be provided for the soldiers he is to conduct to the army; that is to say, that they have a lance, a buckler, a bow with two strings and twelve arrows, and a hauberk with helmets."

Plate VII, Fig. 7, represents a Frankish helmet as worn by the guards of Lothaire. Fig. 8, a sword and spear of the same. See Montfaucon's Monarchie Française, Tom. I, Pl. XXVI, where is also seen a convex oval shield with a spike in the centre, exactly resembling those used by the Saxons.

ALLEMANNI.

This nation of warriors, as their name imports,[1] were also composed of various tribes of Suevi, who united in the time of Caracalla. They fought chiefly on horseback, but their cavalry was rendered still more formidable by a mixture of light infantry, selected from the bravest and most active of their youth, whom frequent exercise had inured to accompany the horsemen in the longest march, the most rapid charge, or the most precipitate retreat.

TUNGRIAN ARMOUR.

A Roman inscribed stone, ornamented with sculpture, and found in Northumberland, gives us the costume of a Tungrian and a Gaul. One is so much defaced that, with the exception of the lorica, nothing can be discerned but two belts, one of which merely crosses the body from over the right shoulder, and the other placed round the neck passes under the right arm. The first of these is a broad belt, and the other a kind of cord, to which is suspended, by a ring on its handle, a curved dagger, with its edge inside. The other is an archer much resembling the figure which Montfaucon[2] calls a Gaul, and round which is a spurious Greek inscription: he appears in a helmet with a high ridge on its top, a lorica, long tight sleeves on his arms, a short petticoat and apparently pantaloons: besides his bow, and a quiver of arrows, which he wears at his right hip, he has a sword and dagger: and just above his right shoulder, as if at his back, is seen an appendage which has some resemblance to a mallet. This costume in a great measure agrees with the following description which Procopius[3] gives of the Roman auxiliaries, "our archers now go into the field armed with loricæ, and greaves that reach up to their knees; they have, besides, their quiver of arrows on the right side, a sword on their left, and some a javelin fastened about them; a kind of small buckler, without any handle, made fast to their shoulder, which serves to defend their head and neck." This shoulder-shield may be that which in the sculpture resembles a mallet.

ARMOUR OF THE ANGLO-DANES.

When the Danes made their first appearance in England they seem to have had no other armour than a broad collar, which encircled their chest and the lower part of their neck, or a small thorax of flat rings, with greaves, or rather shin-pieces, of stout leather. There is still in existence a curious reliquary, which is said to represent the murder of Theodore, abbot of Croyland, and his attendant monks, by the Danes. This event took place in the year 890, but there is no doubt of its having been fabricated long posterior to the event it commemorates, and likewise by a Saxon artist. The reliquary was formerly preserved in the abbey of Croyland, and as it is said represents the abbot officiating at the high altar, with a figure supposed to be intended for Oscytel, the Danish king, in the act of striking off his head with a sword. But as there are more of these reliquaries in existence, as one in the Library at Hereford cathedral and another in the chapel of Goodrich Court, the safer conclusion is that the subject

[1] All-men. [2] In his Antiq. expl. Vol. IV, Part I, p. 37. [3] Lib. I, de Bell. Pers.

intended is the murder of Thomas à Becket. The workmanship is admirable, the figures are chased in gold upon a blue ground; the heads are of silver, and in higher relief.[1]

The Danish swords were made in the same manner as those of the Anglo-Saxons, but the scabbard was more ornamented. They had more particularly as their weapons the battle-axe and the bipennis, the former having, on the reliquary before noticed, a broad flat spike on the opposite side to the blade. The shields are lunated, but rising in the centre of the inner curve, and, therefore, greatly resembling those of the Phrygians.

About Canute's time the Anglo-Danes adopted a new species of armour, which they probably derived from their consanguinei, the Normans. This consisted of a tunic, with a hood for the head, and long sleeves, and what were afterwards called chausses, i. e. pantaloons, covering also the feet, all of which were coated with perforated lozenges of steel, called, from their resemblance to the meshes of a net, macles, or mascles.[2] They wore, too, a helmet, or scullcap in the shape of a curvilinear cone, having on its apex a round knob, under which was painted the rays of a star. This helmet had a large broad nasal to protect the nose, and the hood was drawn up over the mouth and attached to it, so that the only exposed parts were the eyes.[3] Spears, swords, and battle-axes, or bipennes, were the offensive arms, and the shield remained as before.

That the geringed byrne, had become general in its use in the time of Canute, we learn from his establishment of the compulsory heriot or payment for furniture of war as the term implies. Octo equi, quatuor ephippiati et quatuor absque ephippiis et quatuor galeæ, et quatuor loricæ et octo hastæ, ac totidem scuta, et quatuor enses et ducentæ mancusæ. Et postea Regii Thani armamentum, qui ei proximus sit equi, II. ephippiati, et II. absque ephippiis, et duo enses et IV. hastæ et totidem scuta et galeæ et loricæ et L. mancusæ duri. "Eight horses, four saddled and four unsaddled, four helmets, four coats of mail, eight spears, eight shields, four swords and two-hundred mancusæ or marks of gold" were presented by the heir of an earl. "From the kings Thanes four horses, two saddled, and two unsaddled, two swords, four spears, and as many shields and helmets, and coats of mail, and fifty mancusæ of gold." Asser describes the Danish magical standard the Reafan as a banner woven by Hubba's sisters, the daughters of Lodbrog, in one noontide. It was believed that the bird appeared as if flying, when the Danes were to conquer, but was motionless when they were to be defeated. Asser adds, "et hoc sæpe probatum est." He might have observed that nothing was easier to be contrived. Bartholin has collected some traditions concerning such standards, and the raven's prophetic powers.

In Plate VII, Fig. 9, is an Anglo-Danish shield. Fig. 10, the spear of Canute on his coin. Fig. 11, that of the soldiers in his prayer-book. Fig, 12 and 13, battle-axes. Fig. 14, a sword, with a helmet in front; a stone miölner, in my own collection, and one from an antient coin

NORWEGIAN ARMOUR.

It was probably the flat-ringed armour, or that with the rings set edgewise, that was worn by the Norwegians, though we have no where any definite description of it. Snorro Sturlson, in his Edda,[4] accounts for the victory which Harold the Second gained over the Hardrada, by saying, that the Norwegians not having expected a battle on that day had not put on their coats of mail. In that battle the king of Norway formed his men in a long but not dense line, and bending back the wings, he drew them into a circle everywhere of the same depth, with shield touching shield. The first line he ordered to fix their lances obliquely in the ground, with the points inclining towards the enemy, who had so great a superiority of cavalry. The second line were to plunge their spears into the breasts of the horses when near, while the archers who were within with the king and his standard, were to annoy them at a distance.[5] When the enemy had not such advantage of cavalry, the Norwegian troops were generally

1 See an engraving of it in Strutt's Habits of the English, Pl. XXIV. The Hereford Reliquary is represented in Strutt's Manners and Customs, Pl. XXV.

2 Johannes de Janua says, the word is derived from the Latin macula; and the manufacture was probably brought with its name by the Normans, from Italy, who introduced it to the Danes.

3 The authority for these observations is the prayer-book of Canute, in the British Museum. Cott. MS. Calig. A. VII. Strutt's Manners and Customs, Pl. XXVI.

4 P. 163.

5 Snorro Sturlson, 159.

drawn up in a straight line, with one wing flanked by a river, and the other by a ditch, marsh, or whatever might form a kind of protection.[1] The Norwegian forces were, however, generally infantry, and they found that the mode of attack of the Saxon horse was by charging in a promiscuous mass, then to fly off, and to return either at the same or some other point.

The Norwegians were sea-rovers, and this will account for their strength lying principally in their infantry; and from Snorro's account their arms appear to have been spears, swords, bows and arrows, with shields and body-armour.

From an old chronicle of Norway, quoted by Pontoppidan, we learn that the warriors were previously practised in such exercises as might contribute to their success in war. Thus Olaff Trygvason, a king of that country, is said to have been stronger and more nimble than any man in his dominions. He could climb up the rock of Smalserhorn, and fix his shield upon its top; he could walk round the outside of a boat upon the oars while the men were rowing; he could play with three darts, throwing them into the air alternately, and always kept two of them up, while he held the third in one of his hands: he was ambidexter, and could cast two darts at once; he excelled all men of his time in shooting with the bow, and he had no equal in the certainty of his aim.

With respect to the helmet, we meet with the following curious fact in Snorro Sturlson's Norwegian Chronicle: "The sons of Erik Blodoexe having attacked Norway unexpectedly, King Hagen Adelsteen collected a few troops hastily, and boldly defied the enemy. A desperate engagement ensued, in which the enemy impetuously rushed towards the king, he being particularly distinguished by a gilt helmet. Meanwhile Hagen, supported by Thorleif and others of his bravest warriors, maintained the unequal conflict with determined heroism. At length it was discovered, that the splendid helmet was the occasion of so much peril to the king's person, upon which one of the Norwegians threw a covering over it. Evind Skreia, an undaunted warrior of the opposite party, had forced his passage to the king, but losing sight of the helmet, he exclaimed, Does the king of Norway hide himself, or is he fallen or fled? Hagen Adelsteen, indignant at this scornful language, boldly answered, No! behold in me the king of Norway. Evind recognised his voice, and pressed forward."

ARMOUR OF THE BRITONS.

The inhabitants of Britain and Ireland, previous to their intercourse with the Phœnicians, had merely bows, with arrows of reed headed with flint or pointed with bones, sharpened to an acute edge.[2] The arrows were carried in a quiver formed of ozier twigs; and besides these weapons they had spears and javelins made of long bones, ground to a point, inserted in oaken shafts, and held in them by pegs,[3] a battle-axe of flint called Bwyell-arv;[4] and a club of four points or four edges, denominated Cat, and made of oak.

No sooner did the Phœnicians effect an amicable interchange with these Islanders, than they communicated to them the art of manufacturing warlike implements of metal. The composition was copper and tin, the proportions of which were varied according to the object that was intended to be formed. At first they exactly imitated the weapons of bone, and spear and javelin heads, as well as those for battle-axes, were made to be inserted in their respective handles.[5] The javelin, called gwaew-fon or fonwayw, had its blade generally about a foot in length, which was nailed in a slit made in the ashen shaft: the flat bladed one, introduced by the Phœnicians was called paled. After a time, in imitation of the weapons of this maritime nation, the British spear had its shaft fitted into the blade, and the

[1] Snorro Sturlson, 155. Orkneyinga Saga, p. 95.

[2] Costume of the Original Inhabitants of the British Isles, with its authorities, p. 2.

[3] Such have been found in tumuli. See Archæologia, Vol. XV. Pl. II.

[4] One found in Suffolk, at an immense depth below the surface of the earth, is in the armoury at Goodrich Court; others are engraved in the Archæologia, Vol. XV.

[5] See particularly Archæologia, Vol. XVI, Pl. LXX; and Collect. de Reb. Hib. Vol. IV. Pl. XI.

battle-axe was formed in the same manner. Instead of the shield being formed merely of wicker, it was covered with this compound metal, but retained its circular form, being flat, rather more than two feet in diameter with a flattened conical boss in the middle; it was ornamented with concentric circles and intermediate knobs, and was held by the hand in the centre.[1] The Britons as well as the Gauls and other Cimbri used dogs in the battle.[2] The spathæ, or two handed swords, were used by the Britons and Irish as well as the Gauls, and called cheddyv-hir deuddwrn by the former, and dolaimghen by the latter, but I am not aware of any having been discovered. Both straight and curved swords formed part of the Irish weapons, and straight ones, less than two feet in length, were used by the Britons: these have been found in great quantities in Ireland, and frequently in England, but always of bronze.[3] There was also a broad-edged lance, called by the Irish langean, and by the Britons llavnawr.[4] The sword was suspended by a chain, and though we are told, by Herodian and Xiphilin, that the Britons did not wear helmets, yet the antient British coins represent the warrior mounted, and with a scullcap, from which fall the prolix appendages noticed by Diodorus, in his account of the Gauls. The hilts of the British swords seem to have been of horn, from the adage, "He that has got the horn has got the blade." The Caledonians had a ball filled with pieces of metal at the end of their lances, which was called cnopstara, in order to make a noise when engaged with cavalry;[5] and the general ornament of the warriors of the British isles was the torque of gold, silver, or iron.[6] There is also reason to suppose that the Britons used wooden slings.

All the British and Irish youths were trained to the use of arms from their infancy, and their very diversions were of a martial cast. The infantry were the most numerous, the cavalry rode on small but mettlesome horses, without saddles, and the chiefs fought from chariots, of which the essedum was the most renowned: it was drawn by a pair of horses, while the covinus with its axles armed with brazen blades, somewhat of the scythe shape, was hurried on merely by one. Hence, Silius Italicus says,

Agmina falcifero circumvenit arcta covino.

"He gallops round the compact band with the scythe-armed covinus."

One of these scythe-blades of bronze, thirteen inches long, was found in Ireland, and engraved in the Collectanea de Rebus Hibernicis.[7]

When the Romans had obtained a firm footing in Britain, they formed, from the strong and active of its inhabitants, several military corps, which they attached to their legions as auxiliaries; they introduced an imitation of the scutum which the Britons termed Y-sgid, the brazen weapons were exchanged for steel, and the skins of wild beasts for the well-tempered leathern cuirass. This costume so readily adopted, as Tacitus has observed,[8] was continued by the Britons after their conquerors had

1 One of these, found in a turbary, is engraved in my History of Cardiganshire. It is now in the armoury at Goodrich Court, having been presented by Miss Probert of Shrewsbury, and in the same collection is a similar one, on which the concentric circles are nearer together, found in Merionethshire, and presented by Mrs. Newcombe. See Skelton's Illustrations.

2 Plin. Lib. VIII. c. xl. Strabo Geog.

3 One of these in the armoury at Goodrich Court, has its edge remarkably sharp.

4 All these are more particularly described, and the authorities given, in the Costume of the Original Inhabitants of the British Isles, by Major Smith and myself.

5 Xiphilin ex Dione Nicæo.

6 Archæologia, Vol. XIV. Pliny, in his Natural History, XXXIII. 2, in the time of Vespasian, says, "the golden torque was presented exclusively to auxiliaries and allies; none but the silver torque to citizens." Silver not being flexible like gold, the torque of that metal, instead of being formed of twisted bars, was generally a chain, ex annulis singulis, "of single rings;" vel binis, or "in pairs;" inter se cohærentibus, "linked within each other." One of this kind, taken probably by a Pict, from some Brito-Roman, in an incursion of that people into Britannia Prima, was found in the year 1808, in a large cairn, near Torvaine, and is now in possession of the Society of Antiquaries, at Edinburgh. An unique specimen of this shield is in the armoury at Goodrich Court. See Skelton's Illustrations.

7 Vol. IV, Pl. XI.

8 In Vit. Agric.

abandoned to them their antient territory. Aneurin,[1] the bard of the fifth century, therefore, particularizes the troops of Vortigern as llurigawg, or loricated.

Tacitus describes[2] the army of Galgacus as having long swords, and targets of small dimensions.[3] He says they had the address to elude the missile weapons of the Romans, and, at the same time, to discharge a thick volley of their own. In close conflict these small targets afforded no protection, and the unwieldy sword not sharpened to a point would do but little execution. They made use of armed chariots, Pennant in the III. Vol. of his Tour in Scotland has given an engraving of what he considers as a war-chariot drawn by one horse, and carrying two persons besides the driver, taken from a sculptured stone in the church-yard of Meigle. The following was the value of arms and armour, as established in Wales by Hywelddâ in the year 926. The llurig or lorica, the helm, the penfesdin or scull-cap, the pyrgwyn, crest or plume, the gold or silver girdle were estimated on the oath of the parties. The spear was valued at four pence, an arrow at a farthing, a bow and twelve arrows at four pence, a battle axe at two pence, the sword with a hardened edge twelve pence, a sword with a strong blade fourteenpence, a sword with a fair blade twenty-four pence, a sword with a gold or silver hilt, it's value twenty-four pence, one without gold or silver twelve pence. A tarian or target eight pence, an ysgid or shield of blue enameled or gold enameled, twenty-four pence, a coloured shield twenty-four pence, an uncoloured shield twelve-pence, a gold or silver or light-blue shield twenty-four pence.

[1] In his Poems, called the Gododins.

[2] Vit. Agric.

[3] The claymores and targets of the present Highlanders are derived from them. At that time the latter was composed of ozier twigs, or boards as they are now, and covered with leather.

List of Plates

Black-and-White Plates	Page
Graeco Egyptian Arms and Armour	3
Asiatic Arms and Armour	12
Asiatic Arms and Armour	17
Grecian Armour	36
Etruscan Armour	37
Roman Armour	46
British, Saxon, and Danish Armour	63

Color Plates

1. Battle of the Locks and Keys
2. Norman Knight and Archers
3. A Knight Performing Homage
4. Alexander Ist, King of Scotland
5. David, Earl of Huntingdon
6. Richard Fitzhugh, Constable of Chester & Standard-Bearer of England
7. Richard the First, King of England
8. Alexander 2nd, King of Scotland
9. A Knight Armed with a Martel
10. William Longuespee, Earl of Salisbury
11. A Spearman, Man at Arms, and a Slinger
12. Archer and Cross Bowman
13. Eudo de Arsic
14. Peter, Earl of Richmond, and a Soldier
15. Robert Rouse
16. De Vere, Earl of Oxford
17. A Knight of the Montford Family
18. A Soldier and Knight
19. The Attack of the Pel
20. A King and His Mace-Bearer
21. Archers and Crossbow Man
22. Aylmer de Valente, Earl of Pembroke
23. A Knight
24. John De Eltham, Earl of Cornwall
25. Sir John D'Aubernoun
26. Sir Oliver de Ingham
27. Sir Guy de Bryan, & Bernabo Visconti
28. Thomas Beauchamp, Earl of Warwick
29. Sir John Arsich
30. A Knight of the Blanchfront Family

31. Sir George Felbridge
32. Richard de Vere, Earl of Oxford
33. A Knight of the Birmingham Family
34. Thomas Montacute, Earl of Salisbury, and a Knight
35. Henry the Sixth, King of England
36. Two Cross Bow Men
37. Charles the Seventh, King of France, and Joan of Arc, Maid of Orleans
38. A Cross Bow Man and His Paviser
39. Richard Beauchamp, Earl of Warwick
40. Sir John Cornwall, Lord Fanhope
41. John, Duke of Somerset
42. Sir Thomas Shernborne
43. Duke of York
44. Sir John Crosbie & A Serjeant at Arms
45. A Suit of Armour
46. Man at Arms with a Standard
47. Sir Thomas Peyton
48. Henry VIIth, King of England, and a Billman
49. Maximilian 1st, Emperor of Germany
50. Sir John Cheney
51. Knight Armed à La Haute Barde
52. A Knight Armed for the Bond
53. A Knight and One of the King's Guards
54. Henry the Eighth, King of England
55. Two Suits of Black Armour
56. Two Suits of Armour
57. A Suit of Genoese Armour
58. Long Bellied Armour
59. Two Suits of Armour
60. Group of Soldiers
61. Suit of Armour
62. Federigo Oricono
63. Embossed Armour
64. An English Gentleman
65. A Suit of Jousting Armour
66. An Officer of Pikemen
67. A Suit of Armour
68. A Suit of Black Armour
69. Officer and Pistolier
70. Harquebussier and Pikeman
71. A Suit of Cuirassier's Armour

BATTLE OF THE LOCKS AND KEYS.

Plate 1

NORMAN KNIGHT AND ARCHERS.

A.D. 1066.

Plate 2

A KNIGHT  PERFORMING HOMAGE.

A.D. 1100.

ALEXANDER 1ST KING OF SCOTLAND

A.D 1107.

Plate 4

DAVID EARL OF   HUNTINGDON.

A.D. 1120.

RICHARD FITZHUGH CONST.LE OF CHESTER, &
STANDARD-BEARER OF ENGLAND.
A.D. 1141.

Plate 6

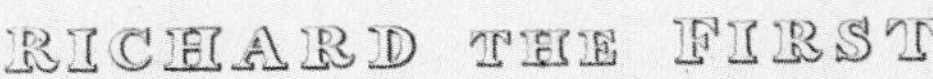

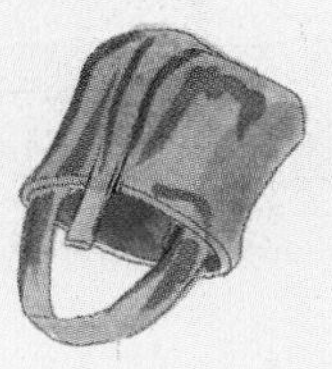

RICHARD THE FIRST KING OF ENGLAND.

A.D.1194.

Plate 7

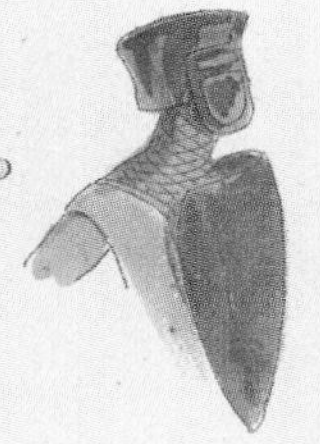

ALEXANDER 2ND  KING OF SCOTLAND.

A.D. 1214.

Plate 8

A KNIGHT ARMED WITH A MARTEL,

A.D. 1220.

WILL.M LONGUESPEE EARL OF SALISBURY,

A.D.1224.

Plate 10

PETER EARL OF RICHMOND AND A SOLDIER,

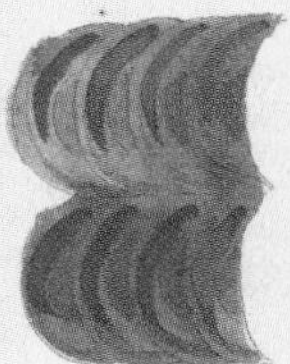

A.D. 1248.

A SPEARMAN, MAN AT ARMS, AND A SLINGER,

A.D. 1250.

Plate 12

ARCHER AND CROSS BOWMAN.

A. D. 1250.

EUDO DE  ARSIC,

A.D.1260.

Plate 14

ROBERT ROUSE.

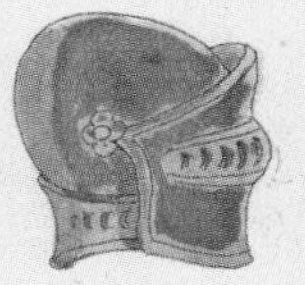

A.D. 1270.

Plate 15

DE VERE EARL OF OXFORD.

A.D. 1280.

Plate 16

Maddocks. sculp^t.

A KNIGHT OF THE  MONTFORD FAMILY,

A.D. 1286.

Plate 17

Plate 18

THE ATTACK OF THE PEL.

A.D.1306.

Plate 19

A KING AND HIS MACE-BEARER,

A.D. 1310.

Plate 20

ARCHERS AND CROSS-BOW-MAN.

Plate 21

AYLMER DE VALENCE EARL OF PEMBROKE,

A. D. 1315.

Plate 22

Plate 23

Maddocks, sculp.

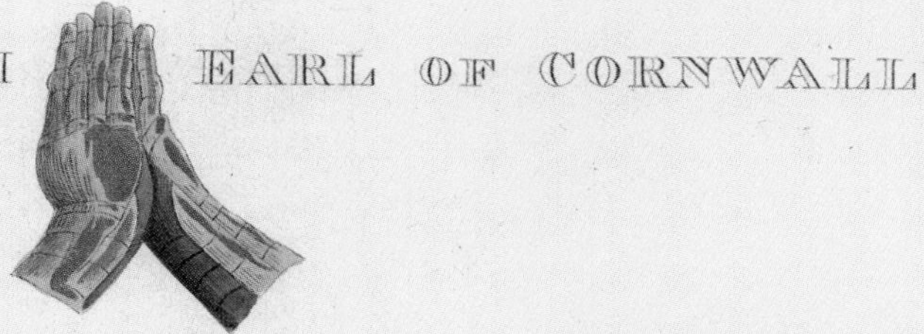

JOHN DE ELTHAM EARL OF CORNWALL,

A.D. 1329.

Plate 24

SIR JOHN D'AUBERNOUN,

A.D.1330.

Plate 26

SIR GUY DE BRYAN,  & BERNABO VISCONTI.

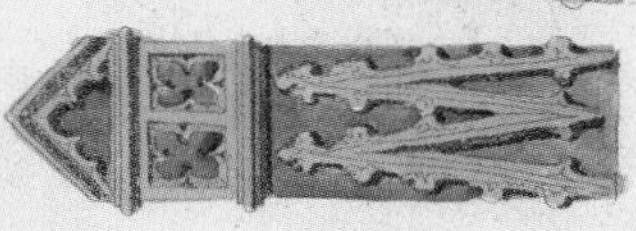

A.D.1365.

Drawn by R.B. C. Hunt, Sculp.t

Plate 27

THOMAS BEAUCHAMP, EARL OF WARWICK,

A.D. 1370.

Plate 28

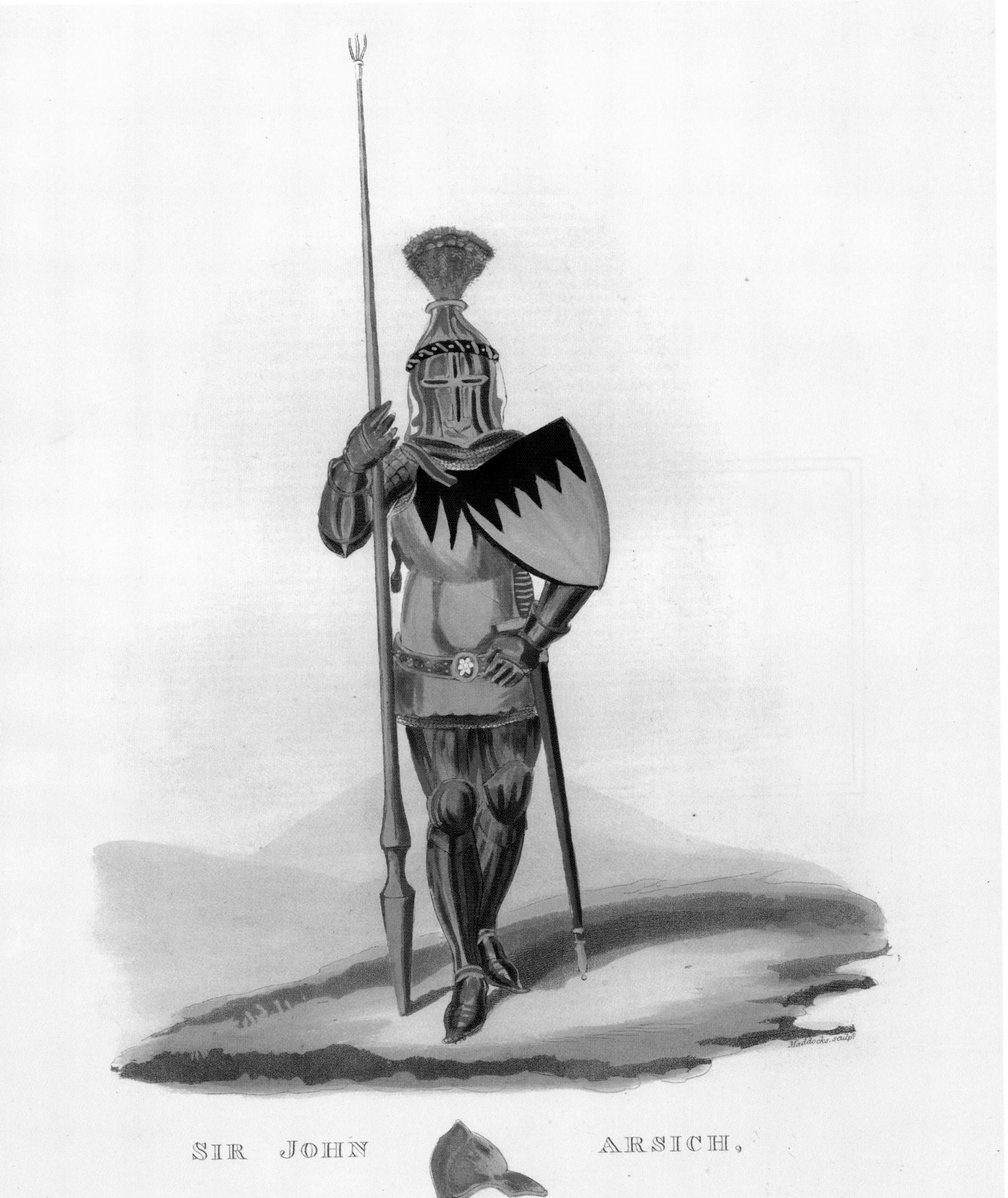

SIR JOHN ARSICH,

A.D.1384.

Plate 29

A KNIGHT OF THE BLANCHFRONT FAMILY

A.D. 1397.

Plate 30

SIR GEORGE FELBRIDGE,

A.D.1400.

Plate 31

Plate 32

A KNIGHT OF THE BIRMINGHAM FAMILY,

(A.D. 1420.)

THOMAS MONTACUTE EARL OF SALISBURY,
AND A KNIGHT,

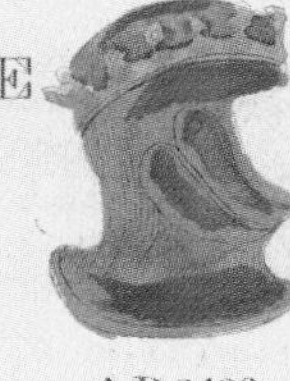

A.D. 1422.

Plate 34

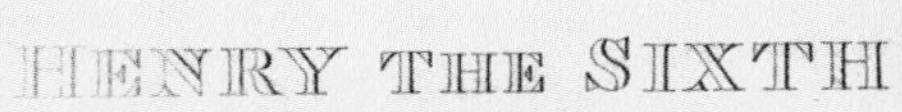

HENRY THE SIXTH

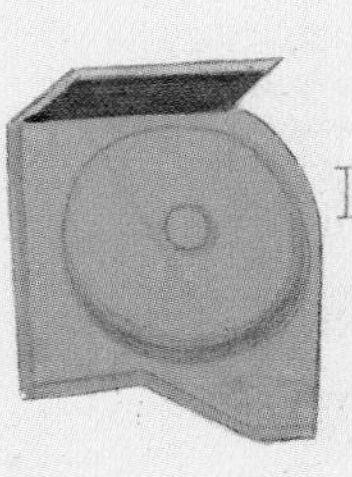

KING OF ENGLAND,

A.D.1422.

Plate 35

TWO  CROSS-BOW MEN.

A.D. 1425.

Plate 36

CHARLES THE SEVENTH KING OF FRANCE AND JOAN OF ARC, THE MAID OF ORLEANS.

A.D. 1430.

A CROSS-BOW-MAN AND HIS PAVISER,

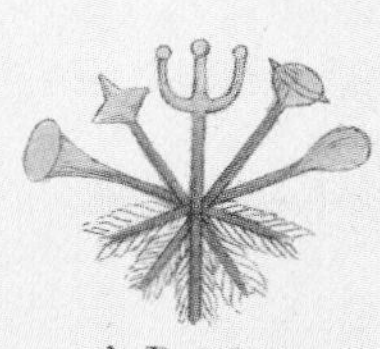

A.D. 1433.

Plate 38

RICHARD BEAUCHAMP EARL OF WARWICK,

(A.D.1439.)

Plate 39

SIR JOHN CORNWALL LORD FANHOPE,

A.D.1442.

Plate 40

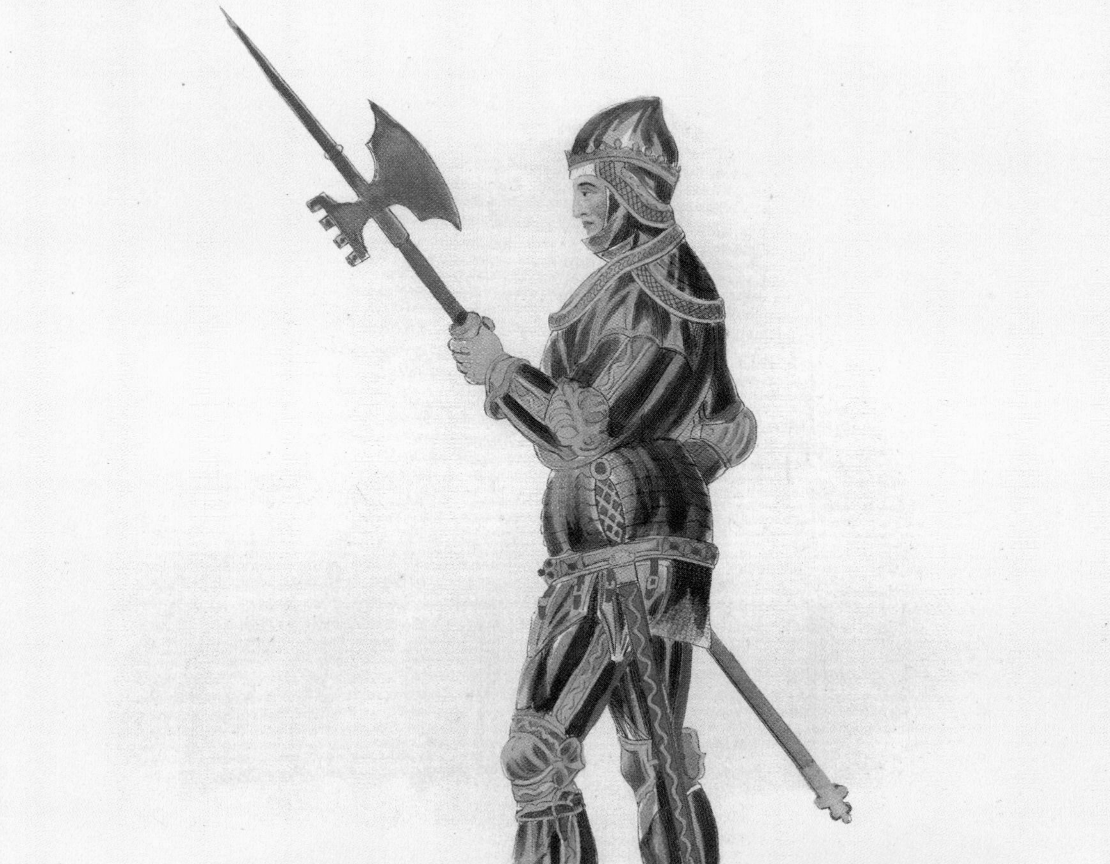

JOHN DUKE OF SOMERSET,

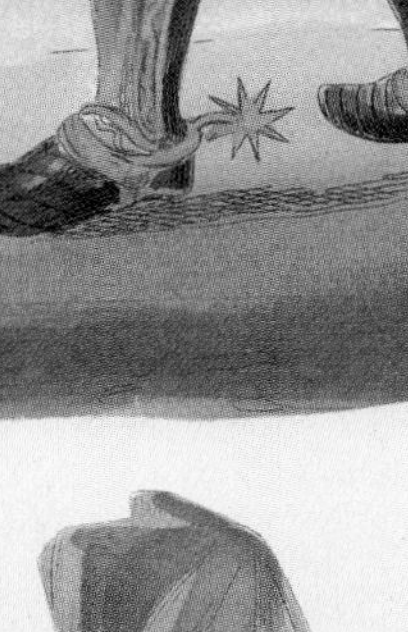

A.D 1444

Plate 41

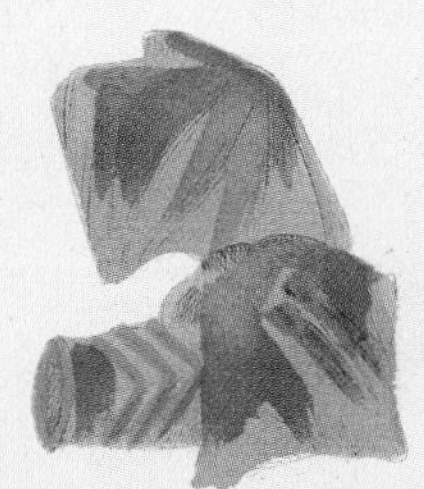

Maddocks, sculp.

SIR THOMAS SHERNBORNE,

A.D. 1458.

Plate 42

DUKE OF YORK,
Father of Edward the fourth slain A. D. 1460.
A.D. 1470.

Plate 43

Maddocks sculp.

SIR JOHN CROSBIE  & A SERJEANT AT ARMS,

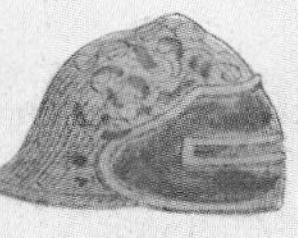

A.D. 1475.

Plate 44

A SUIT OF ARMOUR,

In the possession of Sir Samuel Meyrick, K. H.

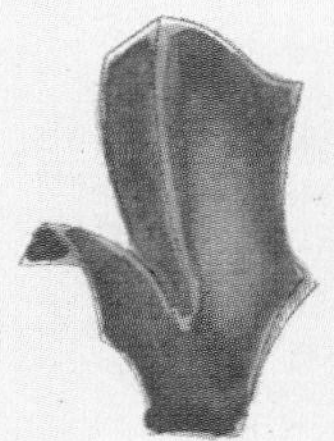

A.D. 1480.

MAN AT ARMS  WITH A STANDARD.

Plate 46

S^R. THOMAS PEYTON,

A.D. 1484.

HENRY VII.TH KING OF ÆNGLAND,
AND A BILLMAN.

A.D. 1490.

Plate 48

MAXIMILIAN 1st. 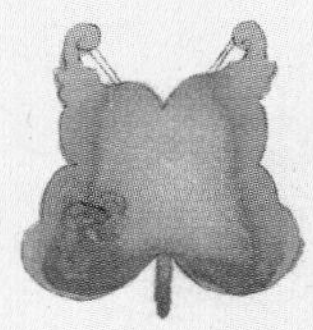 EMPEROR of GERMANY.

A. D. 1498.

Plate 49

SIR JOHN CHENEY,

A.D.1499.

Plate 50

KNIGHT ARMED À LA HAUTE BARDE.

A.D. 1512.

Plate 51

Plate 52

A KNIGHT AND ONE OF THE KING'S GUARDS,

A.D. 1525.

Plate 54

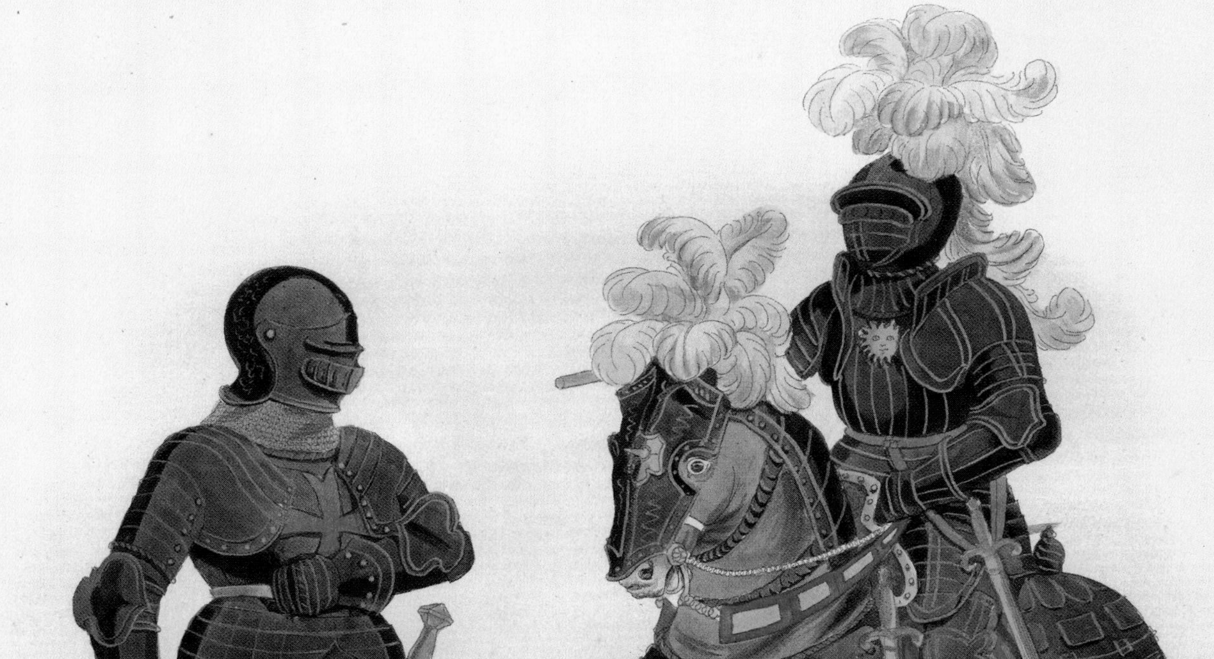

TWO SUITS OF 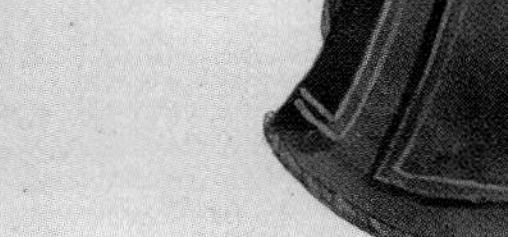 BLACK ARMOUR.

A.D. 1534.

Plate 55

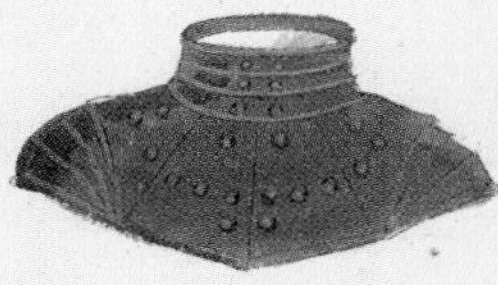

TWO SUITS 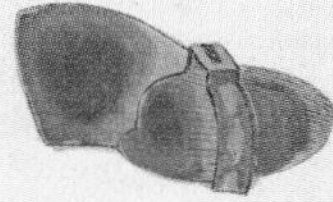 OF ARMOUR,

In the possession of Sir Samuel Meyrick, K.H.

(A.D.1540.)

Plate 56

A SUIT OF 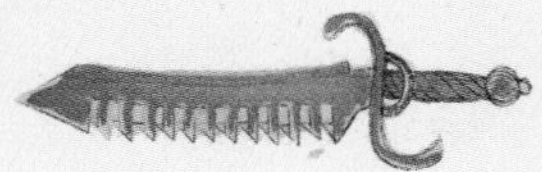 GENOESE ARMOUR,

In the possession of *Sir Samuel Meyrick K. H.*

A.D. 1543.

LONG BELLIED ARMOUR.

A.D. 1545.

Plate 58

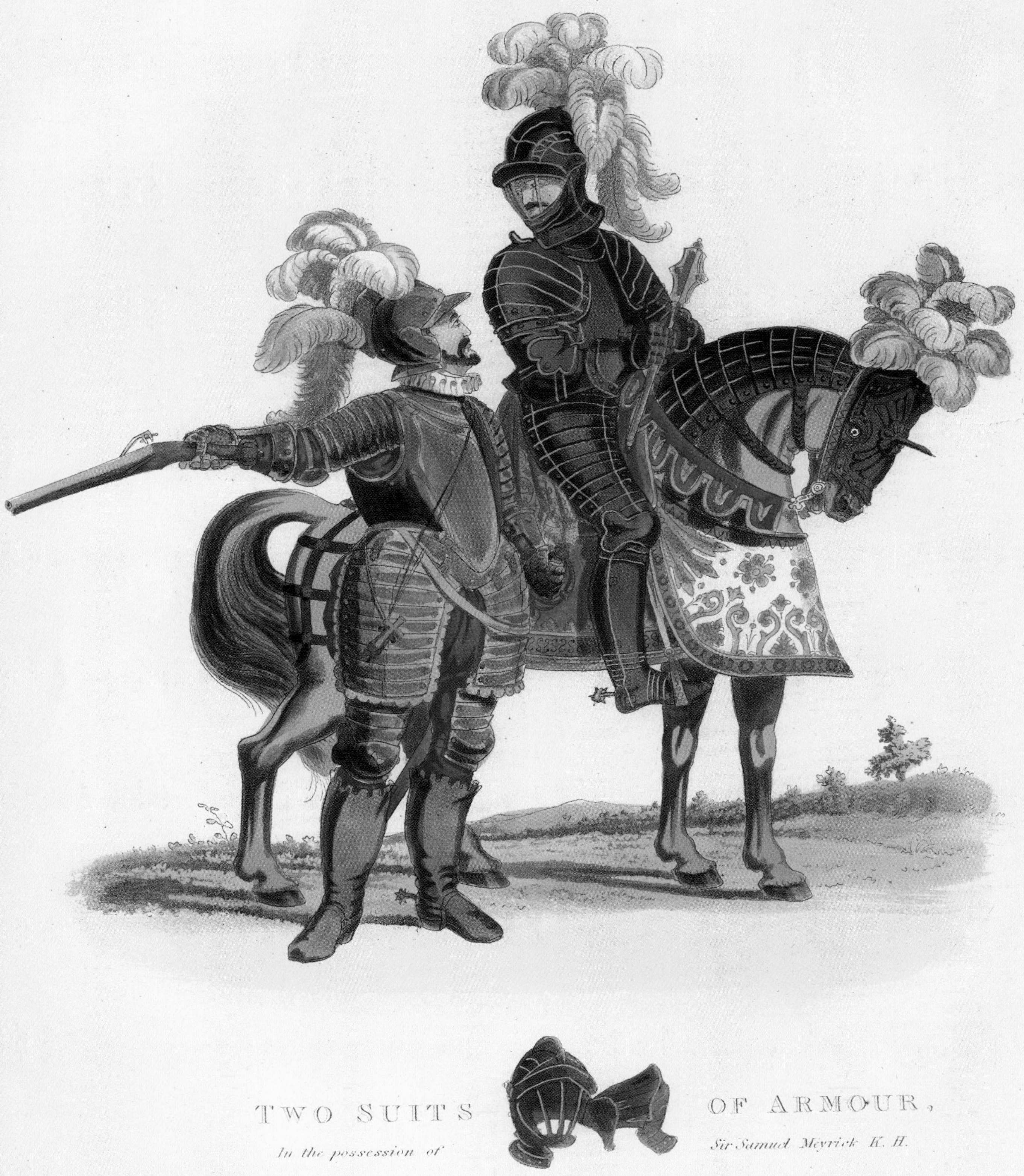

TWO SUITS

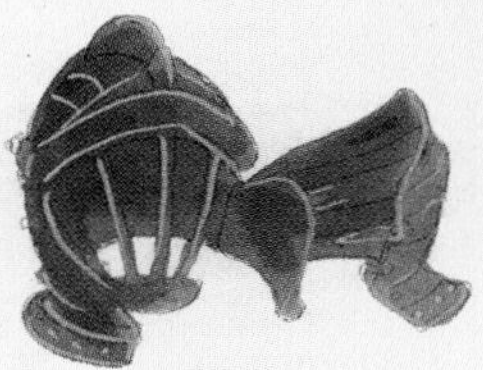

OF ARMOUR,

In the possession of *Sir Samuel Meyrick K. H.*

A.D. 1550.

Drawn & Etch'd by R. Bridgens.

Acquatinted by Cn. Hunt.

GROUP OF  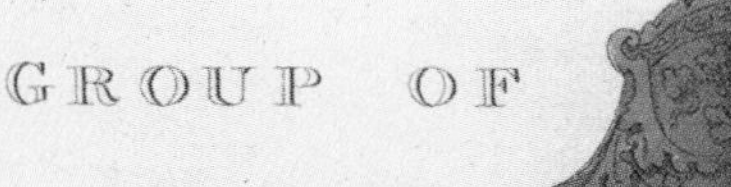 SOLDIERS.

A.D. 1554.

Plate 60

SUIT OF · ARMOUR,

In the possession of *Sir Samuel Meyrick, K. H.*

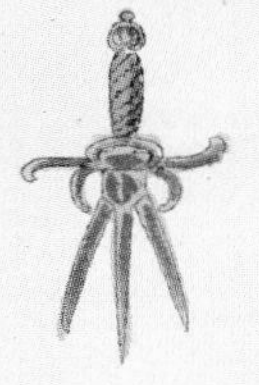

A.D. 1555.

Plate 62

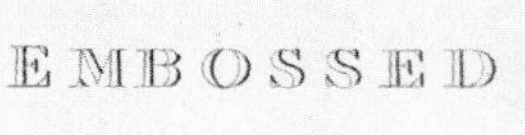

EMBOSSED

ARMOUR,

In the possession of Sir Samuel Meyrick K. H.

A.D. 1565.

Maddocks sculp.t

AN ENGLISH GENTLEMAN,

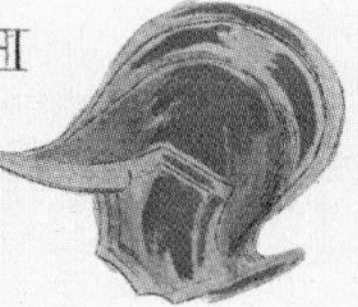

A.D. 1590.

Plate 64

A SUIT OF  JOUSTING ARMOUR,

In the possession of Sir Samuel Meyrick K.H.

A.D.1600.

Maddocks sculp[t]

AN OFFICER OF PIKEMEN,

(A.D.1616.)

Plate 66

A SUIT OF ARMOUR,

In the possession of 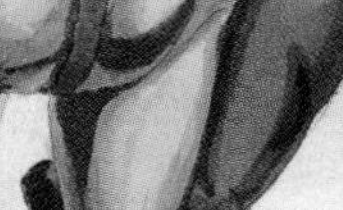 *Sir Samuel Meyrick K. H.*

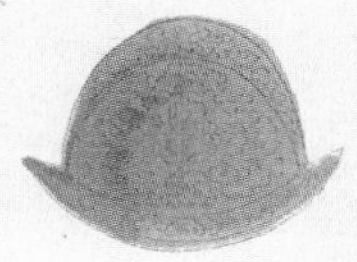

A.D. 1620.

Maddocks sculp.

A SUIT OF

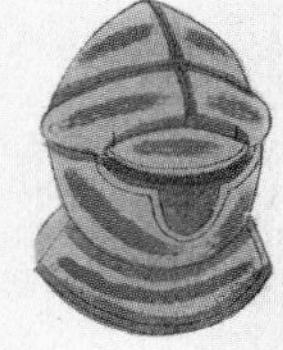

BLACK ARMOUR,

In the possession of Sir Samuel Meyrick K.H.

(A.D. 1625.)

Plate 68

OFFICER AND PISTOLIER,

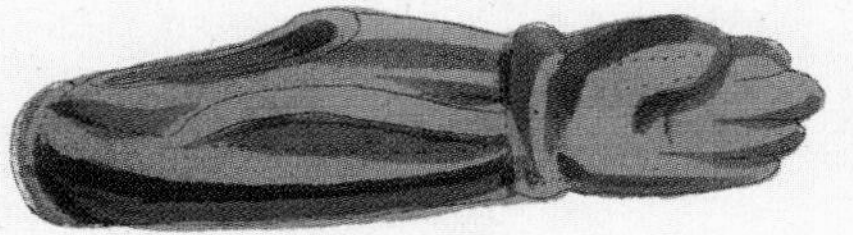

A.D.1640.

HARQUEBUSSIER

AND PIKEMAN.

Drawn by R. Bridgens

A.D.1640.

Aquatinted by Chs Hunt

Plate 70

A SUIT OF  CUIRASSIER'S ARMOUR,

In the possession of Sir Samuel Meyrick. K. H.

A.D. 1650.

Plate 71